SURGEON ON SAFARI

Paul J. Jorden, M. D., and James R. Adair

When Paul Jorden, an orthopedic surgeon from Wheaton, Illinois, decided to work in Africa for a year and a half at his own expense, it wasn't a half-hearted gesture. In the first place, the Jordens elected to take their nine children with them. Then, after being assigned to the Medical Centre at Kijabe, they sent money ahead to the mission builders to put up a two-story dwelling.

From the day of arrival in Africa the Jorden "safari" continued to be a family affair. Dr. Jorden began his work at once in the Medical Centre and found abundant need for his medical skill. For the remainder of the year he was busy both in the hospital and on safari into the interior areas (see map in text). Mrs. Jorden, a home economics major, took over the department at Rift Valley Academy, the school for missionaries' children. Sandra, the Jordens' oldest daughter, also a teacher, taught a class at the academy. Debbie, who took a year out of her nurses' training for the adventure, helped her father in the operating room. The rest of the children also became a part of the mission family at Kijabe and served in various ways.

(Continued on back flap)

Jordens' Safaris

in East Africa

SUDAN

ETHIOPIA

Illeret

LAKE TURKANA
(RUDOLF)

Kalokol

Kalacha

Nyankunde

Gatab
Ilaut
Ngurunit

Marsabit
Loglogo

UGANDA

Lokori

MT.
ELGON

Kepeddo

KENYA

Loputulo

Churo

Maron

SOMALI REPUBLIC

MT. KENYA

Kisumu

LAKE
NAIVASHA

Githumu

EQUATOR

MASAI MARA
GAME
RESERVE

Narok

Kijabe

NAIROBI

Mulango

TANA RIVER

LAKE

VICTORIA

Narosura

Orma Clinic

N

SERENGETI
PLAINS

AMBOSELI
PLAINS

Mwanza

Ngorongoro

MT. KILIMANJARO

Kola Ndoto

Arusha

Shinyanga

LAKE MANYARA

Mombasa

Kiomboi

0   50   100 Miles

TANZANIA

INDIAN OCEAN

SURGEON
ON SAFARI

Paul J. Jorden

with
James R. Adair

HAWTHORN BOOKS, INC.
Publishers / NEW YORK

SURGEON ON SAFARI

Library of Congress Catalog Card Number: 75–41806

ISBN: 0–8015–2147–5

1 2 3 4 5 6 7 8 9 10

To Janet, my remarkable wife, without whose encouragement and able assistance I would never have been able to spend a year in Africa.

Paul J. Jorden

To Ginnie, my loving wife, who encouraged the writing of this book after she heard Janet tell about the Jorden family's Kenyan adventure.

James R. Adair

Contents

Foreword

Have you ever wondered what the daily routine is like for an overseas missionary? Is it all victory, adventure, warm receptions by the nationals? We would be foolish to believe that such is the case. But seldom do we get a glimpse of the actual tasks and activities of the missionary unless we have personal friends who are serving in another country.

Surgeon on Safari is a book about medical missions. It reveals the overwhelming need for curative and preventive health care in underdeveloped nations. It tells of the real hurts of real people. They are not statistics. Such accounts either cause us to shrink back into our world of affluent pseudo-security or they sensitize us to the realities of life for the majority of the world. Hopefully, they will alert us to the relevance of the Gospel of Christ to the needs of the whole person.

Surgeon on Safari is also a book that discloses the ups and downs of a man and his family of eleven as they followed God's promptings to serve as short-term missionaries in Kenya. This story of the application of an orthopedic surgeon's skills to the needs of the infirm is laced with accounts of God's provision as

Foreword

Paul Jorden takes leave from an established medical practice. He risks not only the adjustment to a new culture but also the financial uncertainty and drain of a year away from work. From the very first pages, one senses the work of God in the circumstances of these family members as they first entertain the idea and then make definite plans to pack off to East Africa.

With some variations this is a story that could happen to any of us. We read in the Scriptures that the fields are white unto harvest but the laborers are few. Unfortunately, we act as if God only reaches into the lives of unusual people and decides that they alone can be effective in the harvest. Are the only real servants of God the Billy Grahams, the Jim Elliotts, and other leaders who capture the imagination of the Christian public?

Even posing such rhetorical questions sounds elementary, for we know that Scripture teaches that we are all members of Christ's body commissioned to do His work. Moreover, each of us is a priest with access to the Father. Each of us is able to call on God for the power and resolve to do His will. We are not dependent upon a few selected saints to see God's work accomplished.

But our actions betray us. We affirm by word our responsibilities to speak and act in the name of Christ, but instead we choose the security of silence. We fail to allow God to act through us. The inconsistencies between intentions and actions result in what Francis Schaeffer describes as "*un*faith," or an inability or unwillingness to follow through on our affirmations.

God calls each of us to risk being his disciple in a world which desperately needs God's love but does not comprehend that need. Obedience to that call may mean leaving community and friends. It may mean investing time, money, and emotion in meeting the needs of others. It may mean risking isolation and misunderstanding—even by Christians—in order to stand for what God's word teaches.

What will the result be? For the Jordens, it was a memorable year of exhausting service, a type of "busman's holiday." Some opinions and beliefs were confirmed. Others were challenged and changed as the family faced the fire of life among some of the world's poorest people. This is a story waiting to be written in the setting of each of our lives. Only as we open ourselves to the possibilities that God has for us can we do those greater things which Christ promised His disciples.

MARK O. HATFIELD
United States Senator from Oregon

Acknowledgments

I'm grateful to my wonderful kids—all nine of them. Without their cooperation and loyalty to me, we couldn't have gone to Kenya. And there wouldn't have been a book.

A special thanks goes to my daughter Judy, fifteen, who typed the manuscript with the touch of a mature typist; and to my surgical nurse, Rose Morton, who patiently typed all of my dictated diary notes. And a thank you to Donald Cole, radio pastor of WMBI, for suggesting that I keep a detailed diary of my Kenyan experiences, and to Larry Brown for reading the manuscript.

I'm grateful to the Africa Inland Mission for the opportunity to serve God at Kijabe Hospital and permit me and my family to have a real missionary experience.

Through the encouragement and prayers of Dr. J. Raymond Knighton, president of MAP International, and his wife, Beth, the wheels were set in motion for our term of service in Africa. We were sponsored by MAP International's Short Term Missionary Program. All of our personal effects and household goods were carefully packed and shipped by Missionary Services, an affiliate of MAP International.

Acknowledgments

Amy Anderson, secretary at MAP International, a friend of our family for many years, proved to be a communication center at home. Her faithful letters provided a stream of information to our friends and family on our activities.

Thanks to Ed Arensen, Steve Ross and Art Davis for making their photographs available to add to my own; and to Darwin Dunham for drawing the travel map.

Books and magazines used in the preparation of this book are listed in the Bibliography.

Surgeon
on
Safari

Preface:
How It All Began

If you should walk into our home in Wheaton, Illinois, a suburb of Chicago, don't be alarmed to be greeted by eleven African spears, one for each family member. They seem to grow out of the planter in our reception room. In the living room you'll get another surprise or two. You'll encounter J.F.—Jorden's Folly—a giraffe (front quarter only, minus legs), which looks sternly down from a height of eleven feet.

At first you might think you're in a museum. You can sit on one of two elephant footstools, and you can stroke the yellow-and-black skin of a python. Joining J.F. in watching you would be the head of a handsome black-and-white marked oryx, a large antelope with handsome, almost-straight horns. My son, Paul, Jr., brought down the oryx. The story of the python is in this book.

At the west end of our living room you'll wonder about a huge world map, which covers the entire wall. Pictures on it tell you that we, as a family, know and pray for missionaries the world over. In the midst of the pictures is one of our own family, signifying that we ourselves have been missionaries. The various exotic items were brought back from Kenya by our children; the giraffe is mine, a splurge purchase that I couldn't resist. Little did I know his air fare home would be greater than mine!

We were what is known as short-termers. Most people perhaps think of a missionary as an evangelist who dons a white pith helmet and visits jungle villages to preach a message that, when accepted, will send villagers scurrying for clothes. Of course, many missionaries are preachers of the Christian message, which, when believed, does bring about some conduct changes. But there's a great deal more to modern missions than preaching. Today there's a great supporting team of missionaries who may never preach, and here especially are opportunities for Christian lay people, both men and women, to go abroad (or even somewhere in the United States or Canada) to lend a helping hand, to free preachers and teachers to do their work without hindrance. Thousands of Christian men and women have gone out on short terms of anywhere from a few days to a year or more. They include administrators, writers, teachers, mechanics, pilots, nurses, secretaries, and dentists, to name but a few. I went as an orthopedic surgeon, to use my skills in giving medical care to tribespeople of Kenya—Pokot, Masai, Samburu, Orma, and Turkana, among others. Kenyan tribespeople in the bush country have not been blessed with a general introduction to polio vaccine, and any orthopedic surgeon could spend most of his waking hours straightening out twisted limbs, feet, and hands. If he should run out of cases temporarily, broken or diseased bones would keep him busy.

As a result of my trip, I have gained a new perspective regarding missions and the missionary. Years ago I heard a missionary speaker tell a story that he probably thought would make all his hearers wish they could be missionaries. He described a missionary nurse in her spotless white uniform being flown to the village, people lining the road, cheering. She marched into the chief's hut and ministered to his son, who quickly recovered. Again the people cheered her as she returned to the plane and flew away into the sunset. The embellished story blurred my vision of the foreign mission field, almost physically nauseating me. I sensed then, and learned without question while in Kenya, that the missionary is no snow-white Messiah type, who is cheered as he or she sweeps into a village. I know I was no hero, nor were other doctors and nurses I worked with. I simply found out that missionary work is just that—work. Hard work, lonesome, often unrewarding work. Some people appreciated medical help; some seemed as if they couldn't care less that the doctor had come halfway around the world to minister to them. Aches and pains and twisted hands and limbs— even death—do not seem to bother many of the people. Getting help from a doctor is no big deal to most tribespeople.

Before going to Kenya, I had been well exposed to short-term missions, having first gone on a Christian Medical Society-sponsored trip to Honduras in 1967. I took two of my teen-agers with me and stayed about ten days. It was a great experience, though I worked awfully hard. The next year I returned, taking three of my kids. On two subsequent occasions I visited Santo Domingo, the second time taking several family members, including my wife, Janet.

My call to Kenya came as a desire that I believe God put into my heart. It all began about seven years ago when a missionary doctor, Cliff Nelson, visited us on furlough from Tanzania. Cliff and I had practiced together for about three months. I had found him to be one of the most outstanding men whom I knew in medicine. During his visit with us, Cliff rather casually mentioned that it would be nice if I could spend a few weeks on the mission field with him. He would arrange for an orthopedic refresher course for the missionary physicians in the area. He would have orthopedic problems brought in so I could do some surgery for him as well. And equally important, he said, such a trip would really encourage the missionary doctors. To have an established surgeon visit the field would be a real shot in the arm to them. In addition, he suggested, I might be spiritually helpful to busy missionaries, counseling them and sharing my faith in how God had worked in my own life. All of this really rang my bell.

A year or so later another missionary friend, Don Ricker, visited our home. He teaches at Bingham Academy in Ethiopia. I mentioned the possibility of a short-term trip, to include my family. Don not only thought it a good idea, but his enthusiasm for the trip was contagious. He invited me to come to Ethiopia. However, Bingham at that time had only eight grades. We had teen-agers in high school.

Early in 1972 the Illinois Medical Society sponsored a charter flight to Africa. One week of this tour was in the Nairobi area, and the literature specified that tourists could be on their own when desired. Janet and I signed up, hoping to visit Rift Valley Academy in Kijabe, thirty miles north of Nairobi, Kenya. We found the living conditions at Kijabe to our liking. Rift Valley Academy seemed right for our kids. But we wondered where we could live as a family in the large missionary compound operated at Kijabe by the Africa Inland Mission. Doctors William Barnett and James Propst, the regular missionary doctors at Kijabe, took me to a lot on which there was a concrete slab. Years before a home had been started for visiting and short-term missionaries and their families, but work had gotten only as far as the slab, due to lack of funds.

In time, Janet and I talked of building a duplex on the concrete slab, going to Kenya to live in it for a year, and then turning it over to the mission hospital. I wrote to a number of friends in medicine suggesting their help, but the response was not exactly overwhelming. In fact, I was noticeably discouraged. Janet came up with one of her classical statements, which woke my up: "Dad, if you want to build that duplex in Kenya, then go ahead and do it all by yourself!"

We contracted for the cinder block building, trusting God to provide the funds along with money we would need for the trip itself. As time went on, others did contribute to the project. One doctor friend sent fifteen hundred dollars, given to him by a patient who wanted it used for a worthy cause. This particular gift helped with furnishings.

As it turned out, the duplex became four apartments, which could be joined for use by a large family. The cost, which had been estimated at about twelve thousand dollars, eventually rose to twenty-two thousand dollars. By the time we had completely furnished it, our out-of-pocket expense was in the neighborhood of fourteen thousand dollars.

We now had a home in Kenya. But when could I get away from my practice for a year? Who would take over for me? And where would the extra money come from? God had blessed me with a thriving practice, but with nine kids to feed and clothe my bank account was hardly bulging. The solving of these problems would tell me when God would have us go. Like Gideon of old, I would have two fleeces: (1) a surgeon for my practice; (2) additional funds. And much as in that Old Testament story of Gideon and the fleeces, two miracles gave me the answer. You will find out just how as you come along and join our family safari, which to me is one great big miracle in itself.

1
Roll, Jordens, Roll —
Toward Kenya!

Monday, August 20, 1973, dawned bright and clear in Wheaton, Illinois. Our Kenyan safari was about to begin. We rejoiced that there was no roll of thunder or threat of tornadoes, as is so often the case in much of the Midwest in the summer. We looked forward to our flight that afternoon—from Chicago's O'Hare International Airport to New York City and then on to London and Africa.

Shortly after lunch, drivers lined up four cars—two of them station wagons—in the parking lot of our house. The broiling August sun brought perspiration to our foreheads as we packed seventeen pieces of luggage and twenty-five carry-ons into the station wagons. We rehearsed unloading to make sure all went smoothly at the airport. I smiled as I thought of the problems we had encountered in determining what to take and in trying to keep our luggage weight to a minimum.

"OK, gang," I had announced a few days earlier as mom (my usual name for my wife, Janet), finished checking off items on her carefully prepared lists, "we may have a problem on total weight. We've got to average out at no more than forty-four pounds per person. Let's weigh the pieces and see if we're OK."

As each piece of luggage was placed on our bathroom scale, I jotted down the weight. Then, quickly adding the column, I announced, "I've got news for you—we're two hundred pounds overweight! We've got to eliminate as many items as possible."

My sweet, strawberry blonde wife stood to her full five feet four with a look in her blue eyes that cut like a scalpel. "But dad, not one member of our family could expect to live a whole year in Africa wearing clothing weighing only forty-four pounds! I have carefully figured out what to take, and there's nothing we can eliminate."

I patted her on the shoulder and gave her a condescending smile. "I'm not so sure about that. We're not going to a fashion show. We're going to Africa, where some people wear very few clothes or none at all. We simply don't need to take a lot of fancy duds."

In the spirit of Archie Bunker, I went from room to room, sorting through clothing in each piece of luggage. "Here, you surely don't need this. And you'll never miss this thingamajig," I said, handing articles to the owner of each piece of luggage. My teen-age daughters watched submissively as I went through their dresses, jeans, shoes, and other wearing apparel, consigning piece after piece to being left home. I prided myself in having such sweet daughters. They were accepting it all so graciously, even smiling. However, Janet remained quite unimpressed with my actions and kept repeating, "Dad, you are simply interfering—we cannot live for a year on clothing weighing as little as forty-four pounds!"

Proudly I reweighed the luggage, only to find that the total weight had been lowered just a few pounds. I was not, however, astonished to learn that while I was going through the luggage in one room, tossing out supposedly unnecessary items, the youngsters were carrying the items into another room where Janet was repacking them into another piece of luggage. Smart enough to know I was licked, I merely admitted, "Mom has done a great job of planning; I'm wrong. We'll take it all. It'll cost us, but we'll manage."

Janet inspected my own selection of clothing and expressed considerable amusement. "Honey," she said, laughing, "do you have to take the shabbiest clothes you own? I wouldn't think of giving these things to a Skid Row mission." Never really much of a fashion plate, wearing suits sometimes for as long as eight years, I had chosen my older suits, shirts, and trousers. I smiled but stood firm in my chosen wardrobe. Janet wasn't going to win every battle!

As we left for the airport in the last of the four cars, I glanced back at our house and spacious yard. There was a strange tug at my heart as I realized how good God had been in providing this unusual ranch house built into the side of a hill. The cathedral ceiling in the living room with a family room beneath on the ground level to the front gives the house a three-story effect. It was such a pleasant place to rear a family. And it seemed a shame, in a sense, to be leaving to go into an unknown situation eight thousand miles away in East Africa. Yet, as I considered this, a Bible passage flashed across my mind:

> Don't store up for yourselves treasures on earth, where moth and rust destroy them and thieves break in and steal. But store up for yourselves treasures in heaven, where no moth or rust destroys them and no thieves break in and steal. Where your treasure is, there your heart will be. (Matt. 6:19–21, AT)

For many years I have known this biblical principle, but now it was becoming a very real experience in my life. We had accumulated many "treasures" through the years, and I considered briefly how easy it is for material things to get a real grip on one's heart, mine included. Yet, I was glad that a missionary family, on furlough from Kenya, was going to be living in our home, enjoying it and caring for it.

As we neared the airport I reviewed in my mind the steps taken to organize the family for a journey that would require two plane changes—New York and London. With nine children, one wife, and forty-two pieces of luggage and carry-on items, it seemed that the buddy system would be practical. I had asked each younger child to choose an older sister or brother as a buddy. The older buddy would be responsible for the younger, including luggage and carry-ons. If all went well, we wouldn't lose any luggage—or kids!

For this buddy system, perky four-year-old Jenny, a blue-eyed blonde bombshell, whose main thought about Africa was the excitement that she would become five there, chose Sandy, twenty-two, our eldest. Their physical appearances as well as their determined, outgoing personalities are remarkably similar. You might think they were twins if they weren't eighteen years apart. A graduate of Southern Methodist University, with a degree in elementary education, Sandy had been working at the local YMCA as director of its summer camp program and was establishing a day-care program. At first she had considered staying home. When the day-care program was discontinued, she asked me a question that made my Scottish blood heat up a bit: "Dad, what if I went to Africa for just a month? Would that be OK? Would you pay my air fare over and back for such a short time?"

After careful thought, I told her yes. The eleven-hundred-dollar investment would pay off in some way, I felt. During her college years Sandy had exerted an independence that cut her family ties more than her mother and I appreciated, but now she was back in the fold. Besides, possibly she would see the mission field as a place where God would have her serve him in reaching out to humanity.

Krissy, six, chose Beth, fifteen. This seemed a logical choice also, since they are both quite particular in their attitudes. Shy Krissy, a delicate little flower, needs a lot of attention. Patient and kind Beth has much interest in little people. Krissy looked forward to the trip to Africa, though like Jenny not really understanding what the trip meant. Beth, however, disliked leaving her friends in Wheaton. It was almost as if she would "die" without them. I had talked with Beth about this problem and agreed that if she was not happy in Kenya after three months she could return to the States and live with Sandy. After this agreement, she was willing to go but not wholly enthusiastic.

Our two sons, Jimmy, nine, and Paul, sixteen, paired up. They are about as different as two siblings can possibly be. Mischievous, hyperactive Jimmy, our "mustang,"has been spanked more than all the other children combined. "Daddy," he had said rather firmly to me, "I am not interested in going to Africa. I am not going." I had just as emphatically told him, "You have no choice, Jimmy. You must remember that you are the son, I am the father." Paul, on the other hand, is an easygoing, kind, and gentle young man, well over six feet tall and seemingly older than his years. He always has done exactly what I asked him to do. He was not enthusiastic about going to Africa, I could sense, but a few days prior to our departure, he volunteered, "Dad, the more I think about it, the more I think I'm going to like Africa." I believe he was being sincere, yet it may have been partly to encourage me, since I'd been getting so much static from the other kids.

Because he had been one of the youngest in his class, Paul elected not to attend school in Africa but to work at the hospital or any job where he was needed, such as construction. Secretly I wondered if he wasn't thinking mainly of returning one year older with one more year of eligibility to play basketball on his high school team. I was able to relate to his feelings, since I, too, had entered school early and had competed for a team position against classmates who were nearly a year older.

Sue, eleven, smart, quick, and aggressive, chose Debbie, nineteen, friendly, vivacious, and mature. Both of these girls tend to be spitfires, and I sensed that we would see some fur fly before the trip was over. In the same tone that Jimmy had used, Sue informed me that she was not interested in going to Africa. I handled her much as I had handled Jimmy. Debbie, a brunette beauty, had finished a year of nurse's training and had considered staying in the States to continue her education. Though we did not put any pressure on her to go, she suddenly came up with this well-thought-out reason for going: "Dad, I've decided to go to Africa with you. I do not want to be the only Jorden here in the States. If all of you are going to be killed in Africa, then I want to be with you!"

I'm not so sure she really felt our lives were in danger, but I guess deep in the heart some of us felt there was a possibility that we could meet with disaster. "We could even be cooked in a pot," someone quipped.

Judy, thirteen, chose Janet, a girlish forty-four. I believed this would be satisfactory, since Judy is a diligent teen-ager and would fit in with her mom, a no-nonsense, even-tempered, orderly person. Judy, a shy, cute blonde, disliked leaving her friends, but despite periods of moodiness she was going along with our plan without a great deal of resistance,

Only old dad was without a buddy. Soft-hearted Jimmy came to my rescue. "Daddy, I'll change from Paul to you." I assured him I appreciated his offer but would make it alone.

My main concern was Janet. The excitement of getting off concealed the exhaustion that had shown in her face. She had not only carefully supervised all of our packing but had for months planned shipments to Kenya of the refrigerator, stove, drier, and many other appliances, as well as sewing machines for Rift Valley Academy, where she would be teaching home economics. I hoped I hadn't given her too hard a time regarding the luggage being heavier than I thought it should be. I thanked God for a wife so well organized and so loving toward a doctor husband who could be abrasive at times.

O'Hare, the world's busiest airport, waited like an efficient giant to serve us. As we piled out of the four cars, I barked orders like a platoon sergeant. "Just take your time. Make sure you have your assigned items. And stay together whatever you do."

More than one passerby paused to watch. I may have felt like a platoon sergeant, but they certainly didn't look like a platoon. The two little girls, Jenny and Krissy, trudged into the terminal almost dragging their shoulder carry-ons, which were weighted down with such items as coloring books and dolls. The bigger kids had at

Roll, Jordens, Roll—Toward Kenya!

least two carry-ons each, and, in addition, the older girls carried tape recorders and large purses; they waddled like ducks. Jimmy— the world's strongest nine-year-old, carried an additional carry-on hanging from his front. This caused him to walk stiff-legged and leaning forward. I could picture him landing on his face at the slightest misstep. Paul, like a beast of burden, lugged the four heaviest carry-ons. Friends and porters brought the luggage to the check-in counter.

As I presented my eleven tickets to the clerk, he asked, "Is this a group?"

"Yes, it's a group but they are all my kids!"

"Which one is your wife?"

I pointed out Janet in the midst of the children. She looked almost as young as our oldest daughters. She was slim and trim and pretty; her cheeks were flushed and matched her curly reddish hair. There was a quiet pleasantness about her, speaking of the love that she has for her family.

The clerk must have seen the same picture as I, because he looked at me and said, "You're a lucky man!"

I nodded knowingly.

We went through security check surprisingly fast, considering all our carry-ons. In the boarding area we talked with other travelers, including several missionaries assigned to our flight. One was a veteran missionary who had traveled extensively. I discovered he had checked his luggage through from Chicago to Nairobi, our destination. A feeling of stupidity gripped me; these poor kids would have to lug stuff between terminals in New York, all because I had checked through only to New York. Janet had so carefully organized all of the details of her part of the trip, and then I had failed to make a simple inquiry into checking the luggage. Shades of Archie Bunker again! I'd probably have to shell out plenty when the luggage was weighed for our overseas flight.

Janet's parents, grandpa and grandma Orr, and our friends, stood talking to the children. Grandpa and grandma had not shown enthusiasm for the trip. Both were in their seventies, and I'm sure they wondered if they would see us again. A spirit of doubt and concern swept over me momentarily. If I hadn't had a strong sense of God's call to Kenya, I would have gotten cold feet right at that point. I prayed a quick, silent petition: "Father, I am concerned that nothing happen to these children and to grandpa and grandma during this year. I really can do very little but to commit them to you for your care. I pray that grandpa and grandma will remain healthy and that they will adjust to our being so far away. May our children adjust well to the culture shock. May this be a good year for all of us. In Jesus' name. Amen."

The doubt and concern faded away, and God's peace gave me new confidence. I wondered what men do who do not know how to pray and to commit a problem to the all-wise heavenly Father.

One by one we passed through the boarding gate, with one last wave to grandpa and grandma and our friends.

We had seats together in the big 707. The plane taxied to the runway, and soon we began the movement that in seconds would send us streaking eastward high above the earth. I was well aware that the most critical times in a flight are during takeoff and landing. Yet there was a sense of peace in my heart as I bowed my head and whispered, "Father, we are in your care. Let's have full power from all four engines!"

About two hours later the plane set down at New York's Kennedy International Airport and the platoon sergeant went into action again, directing the family to pick up our luggage. I went ahead. Sid Langford, director of the Africa Inland Mission, met me warmly at the British Caledonia Airlines check-in area. "Dr. Jorden, if your luggage isn't checked through already, bring it down and we will have it weighed with the other missionary luggage. The airline has agreed to this. We have booked some eighty missionaries on this flight, and some have overweight luggage, while others are underweight." A good feeling surged through me. "Maybe I wasn't so stupid after all in not checking our luggage through to Nairobi," I told myself.

Soon the family assembled, Paul and Jimmy arriving with the

luggage. At the check-in counter I presented my eleven tickets to a Scottish lassie dressed in her attractive plaid outfit. With a twinkle in her eye, she said, "Dr. Jorden, we've been waiting for you!" Two or three other clerks came over, apparently to take a look at this odd fellow with such a large family on their way to Africa.

The check-in clerk swept away concern about seating that had nagged me: "We have saved eleven seats all in one section for you and your family." Then she said, "Where is the mother of these children?"

As I pointed her out, the clerks turned, looking at me with the same expression as the clerk at O'Hare.

I smiled proudly.

And then, minutes later, we were airborne, seeing the United States for the last time for a year. As I viewed the skyline of New York against the late evening western sky, I settled back to review the jigsaw puzzle that God had fitted together to make possible our year's safari to Africa.

2

Escapee From Phys Ed

As a family we had naturally sought to become acquainted with the land that would be our home for the next year. We had pored over maps. Books and other literature told us about the land and its peoples, as well as the history of the country and the Africa Inland Mission and its Kijabe mission compound, where we would be living.

"Exactly how far away is Kenya?" "Just where in Africa is it?" "And how big is it?" "Will there be lions and elephants where we live?" The children had endless questions about the country from the day we announced that we were going there. We would be about 8,000 miles from home, we estimated. Our big living room wall map showed Kenya in East Africa on the Indian Ocean, just south of Ethiopia and north of Tanzania. The equator runs through the middle of the land. Kenya's size: 224,960 square miles, a bit smaller than Texas but with a population of about 12 million, or a million or so more people than Texas.

We read that Kenya's life-styles vary greatly. There are big city businessmen and merchants, farmers and large plantation owners, and such tribespeople as the nomadic, warring Masai with their colorful beads and flowing robes, and the Kikuyu, Kenya's largest tribe, rich in tribal legend and steeped in mystic beliefs.

Kenya—land of the Mau Mau, the terrorists of the 1950s, when the British were losing hold and the Kenyans were advancing steadily toward African rule, which came finally in December, 1963. Kenya—where polygamy can give tax authorities fits, when a man insists on taking more than one deduction for a wife. Kenya—home of *posho*, the staple diet that is red bean stew, and where men are leaving their dried-up maize patches and the overgrazed pasture lands to get jobs in Nairobi and Mombasa or to join the army or a police force to learn and enjoy better ways of life. Kenya—intriguing land of great game preserves and beautiful national parks, where tourists see lions, elephants, giraffes, buffalo, zebras, gazelles, and countless other wild animals.

It was to this fascinating land that we were now flying, a Third World country made famous to sports fans by Kip Keino, the great distance runner, sometimes called "God's gazelle" because of his Christian life-style; and to animal lovers by Joy Adamson, of *Born Free* fame. And there are more than a few sports-minded and animal-loving Jordens!

Our flight to London was completely uneventful. The children tolerated the time change better than Janet and I. When breakfast was served, our smallest ones, who had slept as if they were at home, were ready to eat and begin the day. After all, the sun was up, so it was morning as far as they were concerned. The older kids commented that it had seemed a short night!

Our plans called for a quickie tour of London, but I was glad when the tour did not materialize and we were taken to a hotel to rest until our evening flight to Nairobi. At first we were assigned— all eleven of us—to one room. "I'm interested in togetherness," I told the room clerk, "but this is rather absurd." He checked further and found there had been a slight mistake; we were really entitled to five rooms. We caught up on sleep, and, being a family always interested in eating, we ate lunch and supper, part of the London package.

Here we were, halfway to our destination, where undreamed-of adventures awaited us. I had to pinch myself to realize that I was really on the way to a year of medical missionary service. Years before I had not even considered being a doctor, much less a missionary. London was not only a good place for rest between our flights but also for reflection on God's leading in my life.

It seemed that I had been on the move, living first in one place and then in another most of my life, at least in my early years. I was born in 1927 in Millvale, a suburb of Pittsburgh, and shortly afterward my family moved to Ohio. We moved every two or three years, as my father, Charles Wesley Jorden, was transferred to different sales jobs. My older brother, Chuck, was in eleven schools before graduating from high school, and I was in seven. However, I spent my junior high and high school years in one place—Jackson, Michigan—where I played a lot of basketball and baseball and managed to graduate with honors, despite my unstudious habits.

My mother, Ada, had a big part in helping me form my philosophy of life. She was a vigorous, robust woman who in nine months became a ninety-pound near-corpse with cancer all over her body. She died at the age of forty-four at home, and in her last months it was often my chore to lift her from chair to bed or vice versa, a very unpleasant experience. Undoubtedly memories of my mother helped me choose the medical profession. She was a determined woman, the hub of the wheel for our family. I remember, not many weeks before her death, she told me, "Dreddy"—she always called me that, I don't know just why—"if you graduate with honors, I'll be at your graduation." I thought then, "I hope so, but it will take a miracle for her to live that long." Yet not only did she live, she perked up and attended the ceremony. I graduated the latter part of January, and she died on March 10 that year. A devout Christian, she was magnificent during the weeks of agonizing in her losing battle with cancer.

Another person who made a spiritual impact on me was my father's father, a preacher. I remember visiting grandpa Jorden when I was nineteen, following a year in the Navy. He was then in his late seventies, a real saint of God, just a great guy. I really liked to be around him, though I didn't know him well. But as I visited with him on this particular occasion, I realized I was with an unusual man. He talked about his death. He talked about my mother and his wife, both of whom, he said, were with the Lord. This old man walked over and smiled down at me as I sat there. "Son, I am tired." He stretched out on the couch. I watched grandpa Jorden almost with tears in my eyes. I couldn't see him breathing, for, as I know now, he had emphysema and was breathing more from his abdomen than his chest. He was just so peaceful as he rested there. I thought, "Man, that's how a guy ought to live—at peace with God and the world!"

I had committed my life to Jesus Christ as a twelve-year-old, but I didn't have the relationship with God that my grandfather had and that my mother had had. Nevertheless, I knew that God guided my life. I fondly remember my father, who was an unforgettable character, a delightful ding-a-ling. For a time in my late teen years, I was his housekeeper, but it became apparent that I could end up doing that the rest of his life. So I announced one day that I was going to college. I had played basketball in the Navy on the Treasure Island (California) team, and one of the coaches got me a scholarship to Michigan State University. Several months after I left for school dad remarried, which solved his need for a housekeeper.

At Michigan State I made the freshman basketball team and then was invited to join the varsity squad the following spring. But after transferring from phys ed to premed, I found that basketball and studies didn't balance well for me. "Jorden, I don't care if you're a Globetrotter; you have to make up all of your chemistry." I can still hear my chemistry instructor—and my physics prof, too—rip into me when I used basketball as an excuse for not having my work up to date. I had gone on one varsity road trip and had

Surgeon on Safari

missed five laboratories and several lectures. So that was the end of basketball for me.

My decision to transfer to premed came one day in a phys ed class as I was tap dancing next to a tackle on the football team. We were stripped down to shorts, socks, and shoes. As I was dancing next to this huge guy, I looked at his legs, which were as big as my waist, each of them. His arms were as big as my legs. His tap dancing was literally tearing up the floor. I thought, "We are both working for the same degree. His body is ten times stronger than my body, and probably my brain is ten times sharper than his. This is ridiculous. I'm going into premed."

True there had been thoughts about medicine in years past, but no real consideration on my part. My mother, before she became ill, told me, "Dreddie, if necessary, I'll scrub floors to get you through medical school if you'd like to be a doctor." And I had a Latin teacher who, out of the blue, one day said, "Paul, you really ought to be a doctor." At that time in my life, during World War II, I was working in a war plant, and I told both of them, "I'm going to work in a factory." Both of them shrugged their shoulders and said exactly the same thing, "That would be a terrible shame."

I went to my counselor at Michigan State and said, "I want to change from phys ed to premed."

He blinked. "You mean you want to go from premed to phys ed?" He reached for my file.

"No, I'm in phys ed now; I want to go to premed."

"Nobody ever does that, but if that's the way you want it, OK." There was discussion, to be sure, but that summarized the counselor's comments.

I missed getting into medical school the year following my graduation from Michigan State. The University of Chicago turned me down flat, Wayne State University made me an alternate, and I waited anxiously for word from Northwestern. Finally a letter came that stunned me: "Because your application is incomplete, you have been dropped from consideration. . . . You failed to send your transcripts."

22

I discovered that a pretty blonde in the registrar's office at Michigan State had made the mistake. She looked at me with beautiful sad blue eyes and said, "I am terribly sorry." (It was the only thing that kept me from strangling her on the spot!)

I said, "That's OK," and turned and walked out, absolutely stunned. As I walked I got more and more angry and frustrated. Then an idea hit me. Dr. John A. Hannah, the university president, had an open-door policy to students, so I walked over and sat waiting, still boiling inside. When he heard my story, he phoned the registrar and asked him to come to his office. Moments later, President Hannah was summarizing my story and asking, "John, I want you to do something about this." (Both men were named John.)

Only days later another letter came from Northwestern. "We understand that a very unfortunate error was made in your case. We have reviewed your application. Though we do not have room for you in the current class, we will place you in next year's class, if this is satisfactory to you."

I responded that I would be glad to wait. I honestly believe that that clerical error helped call attention to my application, pulling it out of a pile of literally hundreds of others. I also believe that, because I didn't become hysterical or go into a rage, this made an impression on both President Hannah and the registrar. Yet, while I was calm on the outside, I was torn up inside.

With a year to wait, marriage became my next step, along with a mark-time job. I had met Janet Brown at Michigan State; the first time I saw curly-haired Janet she was holding up a test tube, staring at it in bewilderment. I thought, "What a cute kid!" She was a home ec major who was simply lost in the chemistry lab.

She became (and still is) my best friend, a most enjoyable person. We were married in September, 1950.

I entered medical school a year later as not only one of the first married men in the freshman class but one of a few who had children, for our Sandy arrived nine months and two weeks after we got married. In fact, my classmates sometimes called me dad.

23

About four or five kids later, after graduation from medical school, I decided to go into orthopedics. At that time I was in general practice, but I theorized that if the country got into socialized medicine, as many thought it would, I wanted to specialize. On my application to Northwestern, I had stated, "God has given me good, firm hands. I would like to use them to help mankind." The most mechanical part of medicine is orthopedics. In fact, we're teased that we are "sterile carpenters."

After finishing a four-and-a-half-year residency program in the Hines Veterans Administration Hospital as well as West Suburban Hospital, Oak Park, I began my orthopedic practice in 1963, in Wheaton, a suburb of Chicago. I was the only orthopedist in town and therefore, with no one to lean on, not even for counsel, I found myself in a situation where I had to have maturity.

By this time I had come into a new relationship with God and had learned to trust him for each day. Proverbs 16:3 was becoming a reality in my medical practice: "Commit thy works unto the Lord, and thy thoughts shall be established." Numerous times, in my mind, I thought through the steps I would take in an operation and sensed God's touch on my mind—and later on my hands, as they acted out the anticipated action. This is still my procedure; I may go through a certain operation in my mind scores of times before my hands go to work.

My serious consideration of my relationship to God came after a tragedy in medical school. I was assigned as a big brother to a fellow named David, who was a year behind me. He was a great kid, handsome, and I liked him. But being married and living off campus, I didn't see him often. I failed to function as a big brother. Then one day, without my being aware that he had problems, he jumped from an eighth-story window, a suicide. I felt as if I had let him down, for about the only encouragement I had given him was in such empty cliches as, "David, how's it going?" "Don't let them get you down." "Hang in there, buddy!" "You can't know everything!"

Prior to that experience, when our Sandy needed to be enrolled in

Sunday school Janet and I had sought out a church where the Bible was the authority for teaching and preaching. We began going to Moody Church, named for the great evangelist of the 1800s Dwight L. Moody, a church within walking distance of our apartment. I remember hearing visiting British preacher Dr. Alan Redpath, later to become pastor of the church. His message, "The Wayward Christian," seemed to be directed to me that morning. "And God will break your heart if that's what it takes to bring you to your knees," Redpath thundered in his English way. My wife was sitting to my right. I looked at her and realized if something happened to her or to my daughter, that would break my heart. And that's what brought me to my knees, figuratively. I said in my heart, "That, God, I couldn't take. I want you to be first in my life, to be in control." (To this day my vulnerable spot is my family—my wife and children. I pray for them every day.)

After this, I became a serious student of the Word of God, despite the fact I had my hands full with my medical school work. At Moody Church I was given the job of superintending the high school department of the Sunday school—only because no one else would take it and I was young and athletic looking, I told myself. It was here, as I listened to missionary speakers and as we attended Moody Church missionary conferences, that I gained my original impression of missionaries and their work.

At first missionaries seemed especially dull to me. In their style of dress they usually looked like back numbers, and they seemed so out of touch with life as I knew it. But I came to love them, especially later during internship days when Janet and I had a big, five-bedroom house in Oak Park, just west of Chicago. We often had missionaries as house guests, and as we talked with them over coffee I recognized that these rather strange people had a very close relationship with God. Naturally they wouldn't be up on the latest styles and happenings, because they were committed to serving God in another land. So we began to look past their appearance and eccentricities to see lovable, godly people who were a challenge to me spiritually as a young doctor starting out.

25

Finally, years later, here I was planning to become a missionary myself—for a year. My practice had grown to the extent that I owned the building in which my office was housed. Like most medical men, I had a steady stream of patients and usually a long waiting list.

As I strongly considered going to Kenya, I talked to God about finding a competent surgeon to take my practice during my absence. The choice was important, for the practice I had worked hard to build could disintegrate. Through an unusual set of circumstances, I saw God working out the problem. A young woman from Barbados came to live with us for several months while completing her education. She worked part time at a nearby hospital and mentioned my need to a psychiatrist. He put me in touch with Dr. Raymond Santucci, who was finishing orthopedic residency training. On talking with him, I discovered that he had been a student observer in my office a few years before. So, within a few days after talking to God about the first obstacle, I had a verbal agreement for a replacement in July, 1973. The way it all worked out still sends chills down my spine.

As a few weeks went by, it became apparent that getting my practice squared away hadn't solved all of our problems. The cost of this adventure was going to be considerable. Several years before I had invested in some lakefront property in central Florida. After investing approximately five thousand dollars over a three-year period, I discovered through my in-laws in Florida that the lots I had purchased were not on the lake where the salesman had said they were. The lots I actually owned were not as desirable as the ones I had been shown. A real estate attorney advised me to forget it, that I could prove nothing, that it would be my word against that of the salesman. Possibly the company would exchange lots for me, although he had never heard of a company refunding money under such circumstances.

But I was determined. I felt I had been cheated; I didn't want the lots, but I could use the money for our trip. I went to the Lord in sincere prayer about the matter. After writing to the Florida State

Land Board, I received a letter suggesting a face-to-face confrontation with an official of the firm and requesting a letter detailing the entire matter. In writing the letter, I was led to mention my teaching Sunday school for twenty years, as well as my involvement in the leadership of the Christian Medical Society. I ended, "I realize this is one man's word against another. I do not take my Christian faith lightly."

A few days later I received a phone call from the land board. I did not have to come for a face-to-face meeting; the board had instructed the company to refund my five thousand dollars completely and immediately.

This, to me, was another clear indication that God wanted us in Kenya. It would help considerably toward paying our air fare.

But God wasn't finished. He knew we needed more. In many places in Scripture he talks about supplying our needs. "And it is He who will supply all your needs from His riches in glory, because of what Christ Jesus had done for us" (Phil. 4:19, LB). Earlier in the same chapter, the author, Paul, reminds, "Tell God your needs and don't forget to thank Him for His answers" (4:6). And I was doing some thanking after a conversation with my business manager. He informed me that my office building had reached the point where dividends would have to be paid to the owner. 'Since you are the sole owner," he said, "these dividends are your problem."

"Bob, are you talking about a few hundred dollars or a few thousand dollars?" I asked naively. I had left business matters concerning the building set-up entirely to him.

"A few thousand dollars," he responded.

"When should these funds be taken out?"

"The best time would be the fall of 1974."

This was exactly the time I anticipated returning to the practice, a time when I would need funds in getting settled again at home. Needless to say, I was encouraged!

Now, mind you, God did not just reach down and tap a gold mine for me. This money had been accumulating through hard effort over ten years. However, I was not aware that it was available for use in 1974. It was also interesting that my business manager was not aware of my need. But God was. We saw that obviously God's hand was upon this proposed trip to Kenya, even though it seemed to be the craziest thing I had ever considered doing.

Our flight from London to Entebbe, Uganda, where we stopped for refueling, was uneventful. But en route from Entebbe to Nairobi, about an hour's flight, three of our children—Judy, Jimmy, and little Jenny—became ill, though we encountered no turbulence. Just as we landed in Nairobi Jenny lost all of her meal, causing a considerable delay on our part in getting off the plane. Jimmy looked especially pale and pasty. I couldn't be sure what had affected the children, the travel or the very irregular hours and irregular meals.

Many smiling people welcomed us at the Nairobi airport, including our close friends Dr. and Mrs. James Propst. Dr. Propst was the safari doctor at Kijabe but would be leaving for a furlough in the States. He and his wife would spend part of the time in our Wheaton home, while I helped cover for him in Kenya.

It was a heartwarming experience to watch the enthusiastic greeting of the some eighty other missionaries who had come with us on the plane. I realized what a great family the Africa Inland Mission forms.

Presenting our passports brought the same response in Africa as in earlier stages of the trip. The clerks invariably looked with great interest at me and then quickly passed through the formalities of getting us on our way. There was a problem with the entry visas for our children. Politely a clerk informed me that I would have three months to clear their visas or they would have to leave the country. At that time I thought it would be plenty of time to follow through with his instructions, but the weeks ahead involved me in so much work and activity that we had to push to comply and make our year's stay possible.

On entering customs we finally managed to get all of our luggage and carry-ons together, again demonstrating a remarkable sight of traveling disorganizatiὄn. The customs officer asked me if we had anything to declare. In innocence I thought he meant alcoholic beverages, fruit, plants, and such. Little did I realize then that he was referring to tape recorders, cameras, and radios. I said no, and he quickly passed us through without opening anything. Interestingly, our girls carried the tape recorders and cameras openly, so there was no attempt on our part to deceive. Sometimes stupidity pays off.

En route from the airport the children stared almost in disbelief at the sights of Nairobi, the capital of Kenya, population a little more than a quarter of a million. All they saw were high-rise apartments, modern hotels, and government buildings. Nairobi was not a lot different from Chicago.

"Hey, Dad, where are the grass huts and the elephants and lions and rhinos?"

We would see them; but only after getting well settled at the Kijabe missionary compound.

3

Place of the Winds

Less than an hour after our bus left Nairobi, the countryside began to tell us we were in Africa. Our thirty-five-mile bus ride took us northwest over winding Tarmac roads, higher and higher into a magnificent mountainous area. We bumped along past mud huts with thatched roofs and tea and coffee plantations of brilliant green. Small boys here and there herded sheep, goats, or cows. Occasionally we passed a burro-drawn cart. Barefoot African women dressed in brightly colored cotton prints walked rhythmically alongside the road with heavy loads, often firewood, on their scarf-covered heads.

The drive gave us a picturesque view of the Great Rift Valley, which cuts five thousand miles through East Africa from north to south, making it the world's longest valley. Not only were the sights sometimes breathtaking, but so was the ride itself, as our American missionary driver took the occasional downhill curves at such a pace that several times I thought a blowout would render us airborne. Then, during the last seven miles, as we climbed over an extremely rough dirt road toward Kijabe, our destination, I wondered if I, the doctor, would need medical attention myself to put me back together.

Our bus left the winding Tarmac highway and eased onto a winding dirt road. A sign announced that we were nearing our destination:

KIJABE

Africa Inland Church	Life Recordings
Kijabe Medical Centre	Moffat Bible Institute
Biblia Husema Studios	Kijabe High School
Literature Department	Full Primary School
Kesho Publications	Rift Valley Academy
A.I.C. Press	

The bus parked at the office of the Rift Valley Academy, and in my heart I thanked God that we had made it. I was anxious to talk with my children to see what their impressions were. I asked seven-year-old Krissy, "Well, honey, does this look like Africa?"

She looked at me with soft blue eyes and said with all sincerity, "I don't know, daddy. I've never been in Africa before."

The Kijabe missionary compound, home for some eighty missionaries and their families, was opened in 1903, just outside the small town of Kijabe, by the Africa Inland Mission. The names on the sign referred to AIM's various ministries and facilities housed in the compound.

I breathed deeply of the clean cool mountain air, awed by the sights of the area where we would live for the next year. Kijabe is about a hundred miles south of the equator, and here, in August, it was winter. Daytime temperatures were comfortable, usually in the sixties, I was to learn, but nights the mercury might dip to 40 degrees. Summer weather in January and February brings temperatures of close to 80 degrees during daylight hours, though evenings are sweater-cool. The coolness is due to the altitude, for Kijabe is on a mountainside about seventy-five hundred feet above sea level.

At different spots in the compound I caught views of the Great Rift Valley, sweeping majestically to the left and right as far as the eye could see. It is a scene you never get used to. Out of the valley towers Longonot, an extinct volcano, with a crater some 800 feet deep and two miles across. A hardened ribbon of lava, which once flowed down the mountain into the valley, gives Longonot the look of a giant that once terrified the pastoral tribespeople who grazed their cattle in its shadow. In the distance, straight across the valley, you can see Mt. Suswa at 7,734 feet altitude, not as tall as Longonot and much closer, and in the middle, Mt. Margaret, 6,265 feet high. Barely visible as a glistening white dot is the Longonot satellite station for telephone communication with the rest of the world.

The soil, I noted, is fertile enough for growing vegetables the year round. Mountain streams gush down with a bountiful supply of water, except during the long dry season. Tall old cedars, eucalyptus trees, and wild olives sway in the breeze, which some- times, especially at night, turns into winds that whip dust into your eyes and hair and onto your clothes. The rainy seasons, usually in November and April, settle the dust but bring a slick, sticky red mud that makes walking a bit hazardous and sends tracks through houses and buildings.

This was Kijabe, new home of the Jordens. Kijabe—"place of the winds." I knew now how it got its name.

We entered our new home, a large, two-story cement block struc- ture, with excitement and disappointment. It wasn't yet complete, so we determined to adjust to a period of close family living, all eleven of us occupying the upper floor, which consisted of a bachelor apartment plus a three-bedroom apartment. We con- verted the kitchen of the bachelor apartment into a bedroom and thereby had five bedrooms. We had one completed bath with a toilet that flushed only for the person with just the right touch. In addition, we could enjoy a living room and dining room, though initially furniture was stacked in the corner of the living room.

Happily, three missionary men and two Africans were working to put the place into order. The children sniffed the strong odor of fresh paint, and some held their noses. My wife tried to conceal her dislike of the cold bare concrete floors and cinder block walls. She seemed to shiver a bit when a workman informed us that the chimney wasn't quite complete and we couldn't yet build a fire.

A missionary dropped by to give us a schedule for meals for the ensuing week. In each case our entire family would dine out with a missionary family. To me this seemed remarkable. At home we rarely received an invitation for our whole family. In fact, as I thought of it, the host or hostess would usually carefully state, "We would like you to come for dinner on Saturday evening. We wish we had room for the children, but we're a bit tight on space." I couldn't remember our entire family ever being invited out for dinner before, except just prior to leaving for Africa when our pastor and his wife, Chris and Connie Lyons, crowded us into their lovely home.

After dinner on our first day at Kijabe we gladly returned to our new home, anticipating getting much-needed sleep. "Wow, it's cold and damp," I said, speaking for the entire family, I knew. "I wonder if this place will ever warm up. You'd never think we are just south of the equator!" With no central heating, Janet and I instructed each youngster to wear some regular clothing to bed and to snuggle down into two blankets each, which had been loaned to us by various missionaries, along with sheets and pillowcases, awaiting arrival of our bedding.

It was a tremendous thrill to be spending our first night in Africa. All nine kids had accepted our situation without a single complaint. I was really proud of them. With the cold dampness and pungent odor of fresh paint, it was good to have a sense that indeed God had called us to this place. "Thank you, Father, for bringing us safely here and carefully working out each detail," I prayed in the stillness of the night.

At 2 A.M. I awoke. The bedside clock sounded like a threshing machine against the solid walls and floor. Janet, I noted, was following me about the bed like a lizard trying to stay under a rock. The children came to my mind. I decided to check them to make sure they were covered and sleeping well.

Getting out of bed, I sleepily walked toward what I thought was the doorway but jumped back when I touched something that felt like fur. It was our clothing; I had ended up in the closet. These African nights are really dark! Making my rounds, I found all the children covered and sound asleep.

At 5 A.M. I sensed that our bed was becoming crowded. Little Jenny had made her way between Janet and me, and nine-year-old Jimmy was on the other side of me. Both felt icy cold. Jenny was turned at about a 45 degree angle, with her feet toward my legs. Jimmy was fidgeting back and forth. This togetherness, I decided, was getting out of hand.

We awakened the next morning, and on all other Kenyan mornings, to the sounds of barking dogs, muffled by the wind. Men, some on bicycles, called to people they met on the roads and paths. A small boy shouted gleefully as he ran along a path, rolling a metal wheel with a stick. The huff-puff of a steam locomotive bringing a train into town brought back memories of the steam age in the States.

The next few days were free of responsibility at the hospital, giving us time to settle into our home. When crates arrived, volunteer help swarmed in with tools and willing hands. Our stove and large refrigerator were in excellent condition. We now had our own blankets as well as our heavier clothing. One box contained Jimmy's underwear. He had had just one pair of shorts, which he had been wearing since leaving Wheaton several days before!

A missionary kindly loaned us a British Falcon station wagon so we could see the sights of the area. Unfortunately, it wasn't quite up to hauling the entire Jorden family. Its aged four-cylinder engine needed tuning rather badly. On steep inclines the children had to pile out and walk till the car reached more level ground. I had difficulty getting used to driving on the left side of the road, steering from the right side, and shifting gears with my left hand. Since I hadn't driven a clutch shift automobile in many years, the

34

car stalled many times, bringing snickers and snide "you-don't-know-how-to-drive-it" comments from the kids. But we all appreciated having transportation for those first few days until we could purchase a car of our own.

The little Falcon took three of us—Debbie, Susie, and me—to Meyer's ranch a few miles down the escarpment from Kijabe. Debbie wanted to go horseback riding for her nineteenth birthday, but when we got there no horses were available. I was glad, for it had taken longer to get there than I had anticipated, and dusk was settling in. We had stopped on the tortuous trip down, dodging boulders as we went, to view a troop of baboons. Now I hoped the old station wagon would get us back up the mountainside. As we bumped along on the strange African road, my two daughters trusting me implicitly, I was reminded again that this was the dumbest thing I had ever done. My concern quickly disappeared as we came upon a herd of giraffes no more than twenty-five yards away from the road. Debbie and Susie almost went out of their tree at the breathtaking sight. We arrived home safely, much to my relief. "How do I get myself into these situations?" I asked myself.

With the shipment of crates had come an electric blanket, so Janet and I felt more comfortable at night. My long johns helped me, too. I had difficulty adjusting to the utter darkness. On one occasion I stumbled over a folding chair directly in the door of the bathroom. And once Debbie and I met at the bathroom door, scaring her half out of her skin.

Having only one fully equipped bathroom, with only muddy water for baths, we endured frustrating times in those early days, while awaiting the completion of our home. Mornings were the worst time. Once I stepped from my bath when little Krissy burst through the doorway. Taking one look at her father's state of undress, she commented, "Oh, gross, I wish I weren't even here!"

For the first time, all eleven of us were able to eat together as a family. Back in Wheaton, one or more of us would be absent from one or more meals during the course of a day. But here in Kenya we often had all three meals as a unit. At first we had problems; we had just nine chairs and a table that would seat only eight people. Paul and I set to work to solve matters by making a center leaf for the table. The chair problem was temporarily solved by having nine seated while two stood to eat. Needless to say, there was considerable grumbling by those who were standing! Finally, we borrowed two additional folding chairs.

On one occasion our food supply ran low. At lunch the children began grabbing frantically for their share of food. I expressed my displeasure at their behavior only to have them chorus, "Daddy, we're hungry!" It apparently was the survival of the fittest as well as the fastest. I feared that cannibalism might be next.

So I rented a car from Rift Valley Academy to take Janet into Nairobi to purchase a supply of food. She rounded up some three hundred dollars worth of food staples at a wholesale firm, and then we shopped at a supermarket and other stores for additional items. American supermarkets have it all over those in Kenya; here the lack of items sent us scurrying here and there to other stores. Janet and I were exhausted on our return to Kijabe, but at least we now had adequate food for our family.

The kids weren't joking about being hungry. One of the missionary wives, an expert baker, had dropped off several dozen doughnuts and sweet rolls for us. Fortunately or unfortunately, as one may view it, the baked goods were delivered to our home while we were shopping in Nairobi. By the time we arrived that evening, the kids had consumed twenty-two of them. Despite this they ate supper heartily.

Washing dishes posed some problems in those early days, especially for me. With no automatic dishwasher, a schedule had to be drawn up, and to my dismay my name went on the list. On two occasions I tried to shame my older daughters into volunteering for kitchen duty. "Whoever loves me the most will do the dishes for me," I purred. On both occasions I learned that no one loved me enough to take my place, so old dad ended up with his sleeves rolled high, laboring over a huge pile of dishes. The girls were so delighted that they ran for their cameras. At least six pictures were taken of me hard at work at the kitchen sink. It was the first time in twenty-three years of marriage that I had washed dishes. I'm not ashamed of the fact. Maybe I am a male chauvinist pig, but with seven daughters and a doting wife, I never got the urge to work in the kitchen. I have been told that I am spoiled rotten by my family. I love it!

All of the younger kids seemed to adjust well in Rift Valley Academy, a school of some four hundred students, primarily missionary kids with a sprinkling of Africans. They had relatively small classes, with dedicated teachers giving more than their share of individual attention.

Paul pitched in to help finish the lower rooms of our house. There was considerable cabinet work, along with painting that needed to be done, tedious and difficult work. I saw him as a capable young man with the patience of his grandfather on his mother's side. Fortunately he didn't have the impatience and volcanic personality of his father's side!

Debbie, with one year of nurse's training behind her, agreed to help Tuesdays and Thursdays in the hospital. In addition, she volunteered to assist her mom with physical education classes at the academy.

Sandy, our oldest, having her elementary education certificate, stepped in to get the third grade started at the academy when the expected teacher could not come for several months. Obviously Sandy would not be going home after just a month after all. God really does work in mysterious ways, I noted in my diary.

In addition to singing in the academy choir, Beth began helping with a Sunday school class, as did her sisters Judy and Sue.

Our mom, Janet, in addition to teaching physical education, energetically began putting together a home economics program for students at the academy. Our own kitchen became the classroom. Janet had chosen an oversized refrigerator and stove to accommodate not only our family but the home economics class. They had been purchased for us by Missionary Services, Inc., affiliated with Medical Assistance Programs, Wheaton.

Missionary Services also had obtained and shipped eight sewing machines, five of them brand new Singers, for the anticipated sewing class the second quarter at the academy. Prior to leaving Wheaton I had marveled at God's intervention at obtaining these new and used machines. In a small informal gathering where we were asked to speak, I commented on God's provision in a very enthusiastic manner. Janet reached over, touched my hand, and whispered, "Dad, I charged those five new sewing machines to your account." Yes, God does move in strange ways!

Because of my interest in raising children and family living, I was asked to give an elective Sunday school class for high-schoolers on the topic of marriage and related subjects. This was held weekly on Sunday mornings. At the hospital I volunteered to teach a Bible class for African student nurses. It seems that a short-term mission assignment is not complete without a spiritual ministry to the nationals.

With my medical work just beginning, the Jorden family was truly becoming involved in a mission experience.

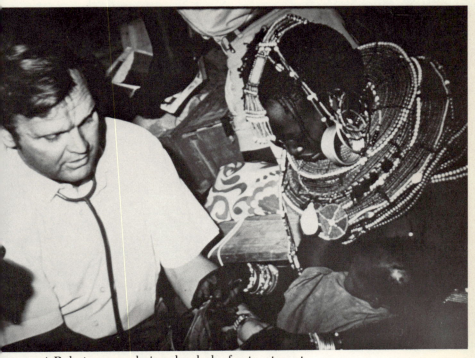

A Pokot woman brings her baby for treatment.

Jenny shares her precious chewing gum. Dr. Jorden attempts to solve medical problems of starving Masai children, while Janet distributes milk and cereal.

The Jordens' cinder block home was designed to be used later as a guesthouse for short-term medical personnel.

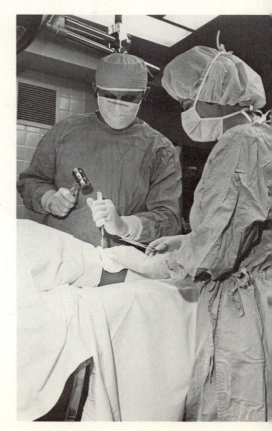

Dr. Jorden in surgery assisted by Nurse Rose Morton.

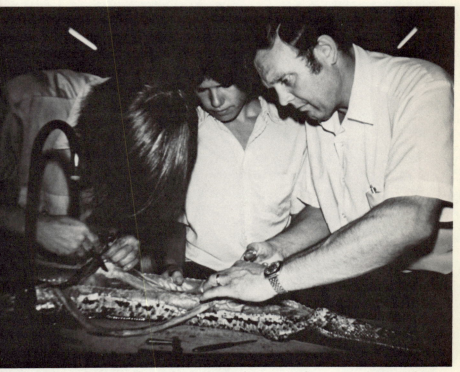

Rift Valley Academy biology students watch as Dr. Jorden dissects python killed in hunt.

Paul Teasdale shares the Word of God with Samburu tribespeople at
Gatab.

Pastor Paul and Jim Bisset at a Masai *manyatta*.

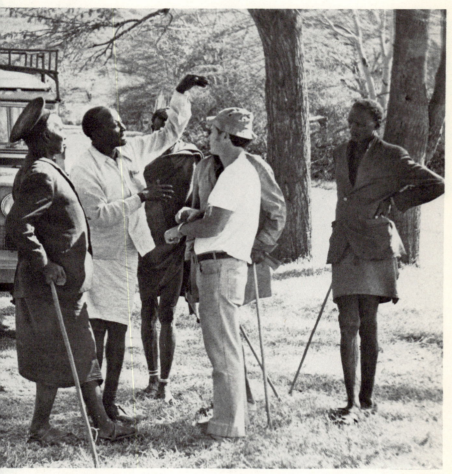

Art Davis talks to Pokot tribesmen, members of schoolboard at Churo.

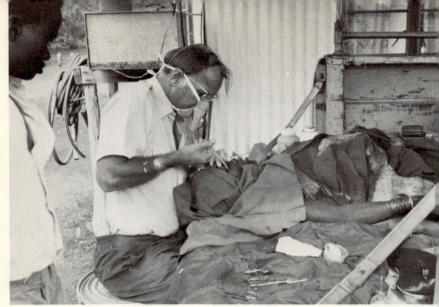

Dr. Richard Anderson, veteran missionary of Lokori Hospital, doing eye surgery on the back of a pickup truck in Pokot country.

Child with spinal meningitis who died after mother sold medication to villagers in Orma land.

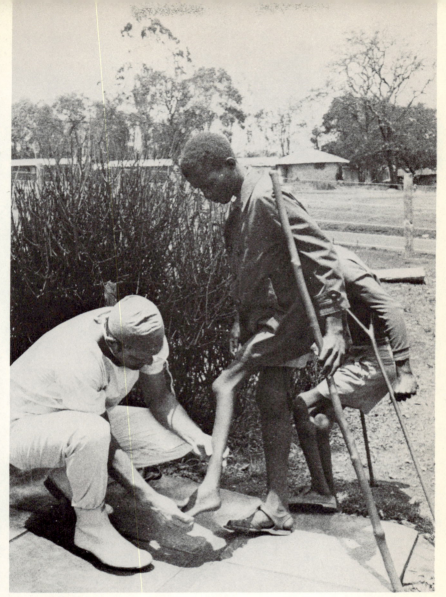

Dr. Jorden examines outpatients between surgical cases at Marsabit Government Hospital.

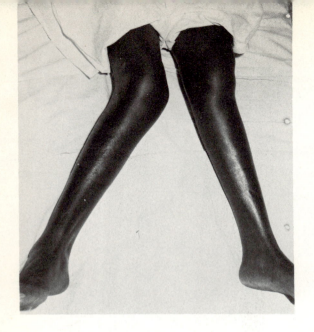

Emily, a Kikuyu girl, smiles gratefully after several stormy days of post-operative recovery. Above, Emily's legs with severe knock-kneed deformity prior to surgery.

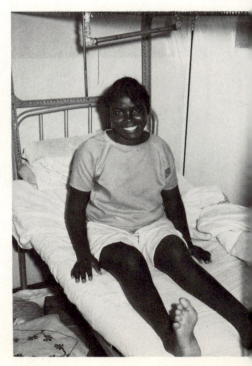

The mountain climbers pause at hut number one while descending Kilimanjaro on the fifth day.

Greater love hath no man . . . than to trade sunglasses and hat with teenage daughter Beth (right), who suffered swollen eyes from excessive exposure to the sun. Debbie is at left.

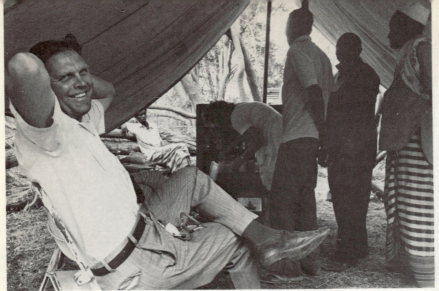

The nurse on safari sees about 90 percent of the patients and does about 98 percent of the work. "I love Africa!" exclaims Dr. Jorden.

"No laboratory, no X ray! What is wrong with this child?" Dr. Jorden ponders as the Masai mother waits.

Father and son, Paul, Jr., share the excitement of "bringing home the bacon." Oryx, brought down by Paul, Jr., provided meat for several days and later the head became a beautiful trophy on the wall of the Jorden living room back home.

African student nurses outside entrance of Kijabe Medical Center. D
Jorden lead these and other nurses in the study of orthopedics and th
Bible.

Dr. Carl Becker and associate Dr. Philip Woods at Nyankunde Medic
Center, Zaire, East Africa.

At Kaloko, Arnie Newman filters petrol through a cloth prior to flying
over mountainous terrain.

Since Sandy and Debbie had already left Africa, only nine Jordens shared joy and sorrow on leaving their African home, ending the greatest year of their lives. Pictured: (front, left to right) Jenny, Kris, and Jimmy; (back row) Beth, Sue, Paul, Jr., Dr. and Mrs. Jorden, and Judy.

4

Work for the Bone Doctor

It was with a warm smile and friendly handshake that Dr. Ralph Bethea, a handsome and gentle man of about fifty, welcomed me to the Africa Inland Church Medical Center. There was a touch of southern charm about this man who, on loan by the Southern Baptist Mission Board, headed the center, commonly called Kijabe Hospital, in the absence of its furloughed director, Dr. William Barnett.

Dr. Bethea was making rounds and invited me to accompany him to get fully acquainted with the work. I felt an almost immediate affinity for this smiling, pleasant man and sensed that I would enjoy working with such a delightful colleague for the coming year. Like me, Dr. Bethea was a big family man, with six sons. He had spent the past sixteen years on the foreign mission field in various hospitals in Indonesia and Africa. In time I was to observe that he is a man of ability, not only in his specialty of obstetrics and gynecology but also in trauma and general surgery. We saw all of the hospital patients—some seventy-five of them—that day just to acquaint me with the types of patients I would meet in the ensuing year. Of course, my interest centered about those with orthopedic problems.

"Here is an eight-year-old Kikuyu girl who is unable to walk due to persistent pain in her lower extremity just above the ankle," Dr. Bethea told me as we approached a small black girl who looked up at me with saucerlike eyes. The area was badly swollen, and there was drainage from an open wound down to the bone. The child's face and eyes demonstrated acute illness as well as the distress of pain. Evaluation of X rays and laboratory work had led to the diagnosis of osteomyelitis of the tibia, an infection of the bone between the knee and ankle. I had only seen a scattering of osteomyelitis cases in the United States, antibiotics having revolutionized the treatment and reduced mortality to less than 1 percent. (Mickey Mantle, the Yankee baseball star of the fifties and sixties, was afflicted with the disease.) Unfortunately, osteomyelitis is prevalent in much of Africa. We scheduled surgery for the little girl for the next day to drain the medullary canal of the bone.

A twelve-year-old Kikuyu boy had the same disease process, but he seemed more ill. The bone infection involved not only his tibia but his scapula or shoulder blade. He also was scheduled for surgery for the next day.

During surgery on the little girl's leg, I removed a window of bone from the tibia measuring about one-half by one and one-half inches. As I lifted this table of bone, the pussy material literally poured out of the medullary canal. It had been under considerable pressure, which explained the pain. I packed the area appropriately and then discontinued the anesthesia.

The Kikuyu boy's case received similar surgery. However, in opening the skin over his shoulder blade I realized the entire blade had been involved in this infectious process. I scooped out a considerable amount of degenerate material, including bone fragments. Next I made a second incision lower on the boy's back to give adequate drainage of this extremely painful shoulder girdle. This wound was packed to permit continued drainage when the patient was up and about on the ward.

The following day my heart was warmed by the sight of the little girl, bright and alert, walking in the corridor. In subsequent days we had difficulty finding her at times in order to change the dressings. The little boy had the same response, becoming markedly brighter, with much less pain in both his leg and shoulder. His grateful expression melted my heart. He was not strong enough to walk as quickly as the little girl, but he was able to get out of bed four days after surgery.

Despite the language barrier between patient and physician, the warmth of human love and concern was quite obvious and satisfying to me. On initial consultation I dealt with two frightened, sick children in significant pain. After surgery I dealt with two warm, alert, and grateful patients who were well on their way to recovery. Their smiles communicated the universal language of love, pay enough for this physician. "Faith, hope, love but the greatest of these is love," I noted in my diary.

Mission medicine, I soon concluded in the days and weeks that followed, is to a great extent surgical. At least, surgery is the most rewarding. You treat a Kenyan for parasites, and he becomes reinfected. You treat a tribesman for pneumonia, and he will sooner or later sleep outside and have it all over again. Treat him for a heart problem, and you wonder if he actually will take his medicine. In the case of surgery, once the surgeon has repaired the hernia or taken out the gallbladder he has solved a problem that won't recur. The orthopedist straightens a deformed foot or sets a broken bone; there's more certainty that the efforts will be lasting. Of course, public health medicine, involving polio and diphtheria shots and the like, is vitally important. But the missionary doctor strikes out too often in treating ordinary illnesses. If it weren't for the spiritual emphasis, acquainting the people with God's concern for them and his way to a personal relationship with him, the general practitioner would likely pack up and go home.

The medical work among Kenyans began with a simple dispensary soon after the Kijabe mission station was opened in 1903. John Stauffacher, fresh from a dairy farm in Wisconsin, arrived in Kenya as a missionary and took charge of the dispensary, giving simple remedies and applying dressings and bandages. The

Africans, quick to read character, took a liking to this tall, dark-haired young missionary. They appreciated his graciousness and enjoyed his fun.

Stauffacher longed to settle among the nomadic Masai, but he knew he first had to make friends with them. They were fierce warriors, and stories of the atrocities they committed sent the young missionary to God to ask him to open up contact with them. In time two African men came to Kijabe with a patient with a running sore on her face. Could the big doctor help her? Despite his lack of medical qualifications, Stauffacher washed out the sore and bandaged it. He was overjoyed when he discovered the people were Masai, feeling God was answering his prayer to establish friendly contact with this tribe. The sore healed quickly, and a friendship sprang up between Stauffacher and the Masai. The local Masai elders sent some younger men to help the missionary learn their language and invited him to visit them. Before long he was able to move freely among the tribe, though earlier a white man would have been killed. In time Stauffacher opened up a missionary work among the Masai. The story is told in detail in Kenneth Richardson's *Garden of Miracles*, a history of the Africa Inland Mission.

A small hospital, begun in 1915 by Dr. Elwood Davis, grew out of the dispensary ministry, and then in 1961 the present hospital was opened, with approximately forty-five beds. Today it is one of twelve operated by AIM in Africa. In 1969 a new wing was added to the Kijabe hospital, including a thirty-bed obstetrics ward, an operating suite, and three private rooms. Plans call for enlarging the hospital to one hundred beds to meet increasing needs. Annually, doctors at Kijabe perform some six hundred minor operations and over two hundred major operations. The staff delivers upwards of six hundred babies each year.

An expansion of the work will enable the hospital to train the medical personnel so desperately needed and attract to the ministry medical doctors who will be proud to assist in this type of training, according to medical director Dr. William Barnett.

Early in my work at the hospital I realized the desperate need for better equipment to enable doctors and nurses to work more efficiently. During rounds I was called to the bedside of a small child and realized almost immediately that there was no longer life in that little body. The child had been admitted the evening before with severe respiratory distress. After examining the child and pronouncing him dead, I found that there had been no chest X ray or laboratory work completed. Thus we had no diagnosis other than the suspicion that the child had succumbed to pneumonia. In the States, emergency laboratory work is done quickly and efficiently. But at the mission hospital antiquated equipment, or the lack of other equipment, makes such examinations unlikely. I found it frustrating not to have all the facilities of American medicine at my disposal. And it was equally difficult for me to accept closing the case without a diagnosis to determine definitely the cause of death. I suppose my intellectual and didactic curiosty would need to be laid aside if I worked regularly in a mission hospital, with its overworked staff and lack of modern equipment.

I determined that, with God's help, I would do the best job I could despite the obstacles, just as the other doctors were doing. However, I soon found that the "bone doctor" and his brand of magic were not wanted by some Africans. A mother brought her two-year-old boy in for a follow-up visit. Previously he had been x-rayed because of a noticeable limp, but she had become impatient while waiting for the X-ray results and had taken him home. Now she was back. I ordered further X rays of the entire lower extremities. I noticed that one leg was actually shorter than the other, and I pointed this out to the mother.

"But the problem is in the hip joint," she insisted through an interpreter.

My immediate reaction was to exclaim to the interpreter, "How in the world would this African mother, who cannot read, write, or speak English, have a grasp of her child's problem?" Fortunately, I listened patiently to her and then examined the child's hip. I ordered further X rays. There was no question that she was right—the basic problem was, in fact, in the hip joint! There was a congenital dislocation of the hip. We admitted the child to the hospital for further studies and mentioned to the mother the possibility of surgical treatment to correct the hip problem.

In a few days the father of the child appeared, obviously concerned. "Neither the mother nor the grandmother of the child wants surgery," he explained through an interpreter. "I want you to do what is necessary, but I must respect the wishes of the child's mother and grandmother."

Dr. Bethea tried to challenge the man, emphasizing that the bone doctor was there only for a few months and this was perhaps a once in a lifetime opportunity to help his child. He suggested that it was the father's responsibility to permit the surgical procedure that could possibly prevent permanent deformity in the boy. Carefully thinking through the comments, the man looked at Dr. Bethea and then me. "It is not my responsibility. God made him this way. It is God's responsibility." And with that he took the boy home.

Another case showed me that surgery can be both rewarding and, in time, disappointing. A surgeon can do only what he can. The results are entirely in God's hands. A teen-age girl from the Kipsagis tribe came to the hospital for treatment of a large mass growing about one knee. X rays suggested the possibility of osteosarcoma, a form of bone cancer. We took her to surgery for what was to be a relatively minor operation. I opened the skin and discovered a bony mass, which I easily cut with a sharp osteotome, removing a sample for biopsy purposes. However, the mass proved extremely vascular, with blood literally pouring out of the defect caused by the removal of the biopsy sample. The only tourniquet available was a blood pressure cuff I had brought with me from the States. No blood had been typed or cross matched, since I hadn't anticipated any unusual bleeding. Suddenly I became concerned that we had a complication of surgery that could not be controlled in Kijabe Hospital.

I packed the bleeding area with dry lap pads and kept pressure applied while I gathered my thoughts. I instructed a nurse to draw blood for typing and cross matching. Asking the nurses just what was available for this problem, I learned that someplace in the surgical suite there was a supply of a paraffinlike substance called bone wax. A nurse found it and, after removing the blood-soaked lap pads, I covered the area with bone wax. Again I packed fresh lap pads and applied pressure to the area. Happily, we controlled the hemorrhage and the patient stabilized. Breathing a word of thanksgiving to my heavenly Father, I removed the pads and closed the skin incision. After applying a pressure dressing, we took the patient to a hospital bed. She was doing well clinically.

We wouldn't have the biopsy report from Nairobi for several weeks. So within a few days I discharged her to go home. But in less than two weeks she was back, bleeding through the dressing. She had bumped the knee, apparently reopening the biopsy site enough to renew the bleeding. As we changed the dressing, I realized that this patient was in real danger of bleeding to death. The previous blood typing permitted us to cross match two units of blood to sustain her life. We arranged surgery on an emergency basis, gaining permission from her father for amputation as a life-saving procedure. I was convinced that hers was a wild form of malignancy to cause such complications.

The hospital staff moved quickly to prepare and to administer anesthesia. I opened the leg at midthigh, quickly dissecting and ligating the great vessels. This gave immediate control of the bleeding stump. We completed the amputation as a usual deliberate controlled surgical procedure.

The following day the patient's condition seemed stable. She was bright and alert, comprehending that the loss of her limb was a life-saving procedure. In the mail that day was a report from Nairobi, revealing that the biopsy showed, indeed, active osteosarcoma. During the ensuing weeks, this delightful young African girl talked with missionaries and professed faith in Jesus Christ as her

Savior and Lord. I believe she sensed the seriousness of her condition.

Typical of her disease, the cancer spread from the leg to the lungs and other parts of her body. Her body weight wasted away as we stood by helplessly. Our only comfort was to realize that this young girl came with an incurable disease of her body, but at our hospital she became spiritually whole. She left her earthly body only four weeks after the operation to be with her heavenly Father.

The case of a twelve-year-old Kikuyu boy brought a great deal of satisfaction to me. He appeared at our hospital carrying his left arm in a very tender manner. His right foot was twisted to the point that he literally had to walk on the top of his foot. It was a result of polio. He actually could look at the sole of his foot while standing on both feet. I examined the lower extremity with great interest after checking the elbow, which was broken. The parents were completely disinterested in his foot, simply stating, "He manages well. We just want help for the elbow." Obviously they were not willing to leave their son for corrective surgery to the foot.

While the nurses and I applied the long arm cast, the parents stood by observing and talking with each other in Kikuyu. Apparently our tender care of the boy warmed the parents' hearts. They agreed to leave their son for corrective surgery.

At surgery, I marveled at the deformity of the body's foot and wondered just how much correction it would tolerate. Removing as much bone as I felt was possible, I casted the foot in its new position. It was not perfect, but at least the young fellow would walk again on the sole of his foot and not on the top. When he left the hospital, the parents smiled their thanks as they watched their son walk almost normally for the first time in many years.

I remember another postpolio victim who was brought to the Kijabe hospital in my early days there. A missionary nurse with her Masai patients arrived for treatment of their various problems. It was my first direct contact with the Masai people, perhaps the most colorful tribe of Kenya. These tribespeople color themselves with red clay. They do not invest a great deal in clothing, wearing only a blanket, sandals, and a big smile. I would later learn more about them on a medical safari. A Masai warrior walked into the consultation office carrying a little girl. My first impression was that this fierce-looking man couldn't have an ounce of love in his heart. Through the interpreter I learned that his daughter had not walked in many years. Polio had struck when she was a small child. Examination revealed that her muscles had completely wasted from the pelvis to the toes in both legs. The best that we could do was to fit her with long leg braces and crutches. Later, as the warrior picked up his little girl to take her home, I noticed his gentleness and tenderness toward her. I realized then that here was a man made in the image of God, if I would but look beyond his cultural dress and mannerisms.

I certainly didn't come to Kenya prepared for an episode that Dr. Bethea got me into one day when he challenged me with, "Paul, want to go along and help us track down a python?" I studied his face as he spoke. Could this be some kind of joke played on new missionaries? "It attacked the dog of a couple of schoolboys, and the tribespeople are scared to work in the area until the python's either dead or captured. Maybe we can take it alive." What doctors don't do on the mission field!

Wincing at the thought of trying to capture a huge snake, being a snake hater, I nevertheless jumped at the chance for adventure. While Doctor Bethea's two grown sons, Ralph, Jr., and Sam, gassed up their Land Rover in preparation for the snake safari to a ravine several miles away in the hill country, I rushed home, changed clothes, and grabbed my camera. I joined the Betheas and other missionary compound personnel who had volunteered for the hunt. Dr. Bethea had brought along two guns, a .22 caliber rifle and a shotgun, just in case the snake couldn't be taken alive.

En route to the scene, I learned more of what had occurred. The two schoolboys were crossing the ravine with their pet when the python attacked the dog, grabbing it by the throat. Panicstricken, the boys ran to the area school to blurt their story to the schoolmaster, who contacted the mission compound. Those who knew the people of the area agreed that they would not work their gardens within a two-mile radius of the site where the snake struck until the slithering giant was captured or killed. Yet, as I learned, pythons have never been known to attack human beings. Apparently these Kenyans didn't want to go into the record books as being the first. And neither did I! I would record the capture or killing at some distance with my camera.

A search of the area revealed tracks that we felt could have been made by a python. We discovered a large hole and surmised that the python was inside. But after digging with no results, we sent the crowd of schoolboys who had gathered to search a wider area. Some time later word was passed along that the snake had been found in the brush. When we arrived the Africans were standing some thirty yards away, pointing to the location of the snake. As my companions moved in, I stood back an appropriate distance clicking my camera—though I had forgotten to bring film. Cowardly, yes—but I hadn't been called to Kenya to rid the land of snakes.

Thoughts of capturing the snake alive were discarded as the men eyed the python, actually a relatively small one about twelve feet in length. Sam Bethea scored a hit with the .22 and the snake writhed violently, scattering nearby onlookers. Quickly someone raised the shotgun and fired at close range. The Africans cheered as they moved in for a closer look at the snake, with the bulge in its midsection that was the undigested dog.

We brought the snake to the school, where Ralph Bethea was the biology teacher. Would I dissect the snake for the students, he asked me. I accepted the dubious honor without hesitation. After all, how many orthopedic surgeons have dissected a python to remove a dog? (After my return to Africa, I asked this rhetorical question at a medical meeting. The general response seemed to be, "Who cares?")

The dissection revealed the remarkable elasticity of a python. The jaws had dislocated to permit the dog, which weighed about forty pounds, to pass headfirst into the tiny, elastic esophogus (normally the diameter of a pencil) and on to the stomach. Partial digestion had occurred, but otherwise the dog was still intact. The .22 bullet, fired first, had either killed the python immediately, or it would have died quickly, for the bullet had cut right through the windpipe. The shotgun blasts served only to pepper the colorful skin with holes.

The biology class later presented the python skin to me for tanning as an expression of their appreciation for my dissection and accompanying lecture identifying all of the structures of the snake. That skin is now draped over the top of our grand piano in Wheaton.

One day a radio call introduced me to Tenwick Hospital, another ministry about 180 miles north of Kijabe. Dr. Ernest Steury needed my help with a difficult case. I had met him briefly sometime earlier, and he had impressed me immediately as a sincere, dedicated man who loved God and people. I was most anxious to accommodate him. Typical of the missionary attitude of being ready to meet needs, Jim Bigley of the RVA staff agreed to drive me to Tenwick. Jim and his wife, a missionary nurse, had once served near Tenwick at Litein Clinic and knew the location of this hard to find mountain hospital.

Prior to starting our five-and-a-half-hour drive, Jim paused for a word of prayer. He committed our travel to God's hands. I was impressed with his sincerity and learned from this that any Christian should pray before undertaking an automobile trip—especially in Kenya! You can never be sure of the other driver, who may take his half of the road in the middle. Or you may suddenly come upon an abandoned vehicle. Or maybe you'll round a turn only to find a herd of zebras or impalas blocking the way.

Most of the trip was on Tarmac, through open areas and mountainous terrain with multiple shades of green. I never tired of the magnificent scenery of blue skies with huge white cumulus clouds accented by the lovely greens. Rainfall in that area is frequent, giving a plush vegetation as far as the eye can see. Jim Bigley pointed out many of the sights and identified certain vegetation as we bounced along in his European car.

Dr. Steury greeted us with a hearty handshake. "We have 135 beds here," he pointed out as we made the rounds, "but you'll often find two patients to a bed and sometimes a third patient underneath." The hospital is attended by Dr. Steury and several missionary nurses. He asked me to see a man with a three-year-old fractured femur. It had angulated badly, with signs of long-standing infection. An intramedullary rod would be necessary, along with the removal of several pieces of dead bone. The case was scheduled for the next day.

The surgical procedure went well, although we lacked many orthopedic instruments. The angulation of the fracture, along with the chronic infection, had caused scarring about the fracture site. This caused me some anxiety, since large blood vessels are in the area. Should we tear or cut one of these vessels, serious hemorrhage could result. Again I saw why missionary doctors pause to pray before surgery. I opened the skin over the fracture and drove the intramedullary rod down through the bone and out of the buttock and then back into the other section of the bone to connect the break. But it happened that the intramedullary rod was two inches too long, causing it to protrude outside the skin of the buttock. Looking at Dr. Steury, I casually asked, "Do you have a hacksaw?"

His eyes above his mask almost laughed with astonishment. "Yes, in my garage!"

"Fine, if you'll break scrub and sterilize the hacksaw, I think we'll have this problem licked."

My request for a hacksaw in surgery may seem strange. Twelve years ago I had begun my practice in a small hospital in a generally rural area. We did not have the niceties of a large hospital. One of the problems I faced in those days was cutting intramedullary rods, which come in forty-eight sizes. I had learned through an old country orthopedic surgeon that these rods could indeed be sawed off with a hacksaw, provided it was made entirely of metal, making thorough sterilization possible.

Dr. Steury soon arrived with his hacksaw. I grasped the rod with a pair of pliers, sawing off about two inches of the rod and making it fit perfectly. My heart was warm with the realization of how completely God prepares people for the plan that he has for their lives. In my early practice in a country hospital in Illinois I had learned a technique that would prove helpful in a remote hospital in Kenya.

Before leaving Tenwick Hospital, I sat down and chatted with Dr. Steury for several hours, reviewing the orthopedic problems he had encountered in the past few weeks at his hospital. It was a real privilege for me to review for him some orthopedic principles and tricks of the trade. There was deep satisfaction that I could help this dedicated man of God in some way with his orthopedic cases.

When I returned home I got a warm welcome, the little ones running into my arms. At home, however, I was no longer Dr. Jorden the bone doctor, but Mr. Fix-it, or just plain old dad. I remember when Janet arranged for three Ping-Pong tables to be built by Tony Dickens, of the RVA staff, to use as sewing tables as well as for Ping-Pong. Debbie, Paul and I decided to paint these tables. We had a great time chatting about many different things while glopping on green and white paint. It is always refreshing to me to have a task that does not involve decision making in life-or-death situations. I'm not sure people realize the price that is paid by a conscientious physician or surgeon. It's refreshing to me to be able just to dink around with a couple of my kids.

But then there are those difficult tasks that come my way at home. Beth, our fifteen-year-old, dumped a pair of lace panties in my lap. "Got a problem, dad. Can you help?" Somehow one of her fancy rings had become entwined in the lace. She was concerned that the two be separated but that no defect be made in the panties. Finding a bright light and adjusting my reading glasses, I spent considerable time teasing the various strands of lace from her fancy ornamental ring, finally freeing the ring without damaging the panties. Somehow this problem did not seem as important to me as it did to Beth, but Beth was important to me. Her "thanks, dad" was better than cash for a complicated orthopedic procedure.

Jenny, our youngest, came to me with a great problem in her life. Her Raggedy Ann doll had had its clothes dismantled, and she was unable to dress it. I spent considerable time trying to put this doll back together again. She gave me the payment of all payments as I handed Raggedy Ann back with its clothes all in order. "Thank you, daddy!" she squealed, giving me a big hug and kiss on the neck.

Home problems could, on occasion, take precedence over my hospital practice. One morning as I was leaving for a day's work, Janet rushed to me with a distressed look. "Dad, the washing machine wringer has broken. Washing must be done today. Please see what you can do before you leave."

As I struggled with the puzzle of how to fix an old-fashioned washing machine wringer, a missionary appeared at the door—almost like an angel. When he saw my dilemma, he rolled up his sleeves and together we solved the problem. I was nearly two hours late getting to the hospital; my friend's schedule had been completely disrupted. Yet he accepted the delay graciously, without murmur. "Jorden," I told myself, "you must learn not only to live one day at a time but one event at a time. There are no accidents in the life of a true believer in Jesus Christ. All of these interruptions and unpleasantries are permitted by God to teach us something. That something in my life is patience." Lord, teach me patience . . . right now!

Earlier, just teaching my older daughters to use an old-fashioned washer had brought back warm memories and proved a good experience in itself. My daughters did not even know what the washing machine was when they first saw it—it was so different from the automatic washer in Wheaton. I had experienced using an old wringer-type washer as a teen-ager; I helped do the family washing and ironing while my mother was dying of cancer. My wife also had used this type of machine while I was in medical school. So it was fun taking each of my older daughters aside with a load of their washing to teach them how to use this antique washer.

In Kenya we celebrated birthdays and our wedding anniversary with all the fanfare that we had in Wheaton—almost. Remarkable Janet managed to have a token gift for each occasion, along with a cake and candles. We sang "Happy Birthday" enthusiastically, making up in volume what we lacked in harmony.

When it came to our twenty-third wedding anniversary I couldn't run down to a nearby card shop, so I tried my hand at a work of art. Taking multicolored pens and a piece of paper, great inspiration led to, "Roses are red / violets are blue / Man, am I glad that I married you! All my love, Dad." The small kids thought this was a great anniversary card, but the teen-age girls called it corny. Janet's smile didn't really let me know what she thought of my card. But deep in her heart I knew that she knew how much I loved her.

Jenny's fifth birthday was complete with our song, cake, and candles. And to top things off we made Jenny's eyes sparkle by producing her favorite sugarcoated cereal, devoured with great gusto by the birthday girl. There seems to be no question in our children's minds that their daily bread will be supplied by their earthly parents. I noted that we feed, clothe, chasten, and love them every day. There seemed to be no thought on their part that their needs would not be met. I wrote in my diary, "It seems sad that Christian adults with a heavenly Father so often worry and are anxious about their needs. I must learn to take no thought for the morrow."

There were indeed times when my only sources of provision and peace were in God. One instance involved little Jenny. After the python was killed, while I was dissecting it for the RVA science class, Jenny, who had been watching, moved on to look at rats that were in the classroom as part of a special study. Somehow she and five others, including a teacher, were bitten by these rats.

Dr. Bethea and I were not particularly concerned until the next day revealed that one rat had died and the others had eaten it. We felt this was unusual behavior even for rats. Possibly they had rabies! The four kids and teacher were started on antirabies vaccine about their umbilicus (belly buttons). Jenny was brave for the first two shots, not crying at all. However, the second shot produced a reaction, causing her stomach to look much like a large boil. Aware that rabies in a human is almost universally fatal, I had a major decision on my hands. With considerable prayer, I elected to discontinue the rabies shots on my daughter. The next few days brought many moments of anguish as I came in contact with this little girl. "Oh God, don't let my decision be in error."

Happily, the rats did not prove to have rabies, and all turned out well. Later I learned that it isn't unusual for rats to devour a dead rat.

How important it is that my own children receive the best medical attention. I could sympathize better with Africans whose children were suffering with disease and afflictions. In time I would have the opportunity to go on my first medical safari, apart from the trek to Tenwick Hospital, to minister to the needs of more of these people.

5

On Safari to NFD

The short-term medical missionary, like the regular staff physicians at Kijabe, doesn't wait for patients to come to him. A bit like the country doctor of old, the missionary doctor in Kenya goes calling. But unlike the country doctor, whose house calls usually took him only a few miles, the medical missionary may find himself flying hundreds of miles and bumping additional miles over almost impossible roads to treat tribespeople in remote areas. Most visits are to small mission clinics, operated by a missionary nurse or even a regular missionary who has learned first aid and a few simple remedies.

My first outpost assignment was to take me into the NFD—the Northern Frontier District, surrounding 185-mile Lake Rudolf (now named Lake Turkana) and bordered on the north by Ethiopia. The area is inhabited by such tribespeople as the Samburu, Turkana, Boran, and Rendile, who eke out an existence on the dry, bush-covered plains and in the highlands. My companion for the medical safari was to be Dr. Jon Allen, a first-term general doctor from Australia. Our destination: Gatab, a village two-and-a-half hours away by air in the mountains just east of Lake Rudolf.

We arrived early on a morning in September at Wilson Airport in Nairobi and were met by Arnie Newman, a pleasant, round-faced man whom I judged to be in his late thirties. An American, Arnie was an AIM missionary on loan then to British Missionary Aviation Fellowship. More recently he has become operations director of AIM-AIR, the new air link between the many AIM stations scattered over Kenya and other East African countries.

While the single-engine red and white Cessna 206 warmed up, Arnie turned to us. "Let's pause and ask God's guidance. Dear heavenly Father," he began, "we ask you for guidance and ask you to manifest your presence on this flight and throughout this day. May each opportunity be recognized and met in the love of God. May we have a good day in the Lord . . . "

Is it prayer that has given these missionary pilots such an excellent record through the years, I asked myself. Despite the fact that I knew Arnie to be a very capable pilot, his prayer did give a sense of great confidence as we headed for the Northern Frontier.

Our plane at times bumped along high in the blue African sky, graced here and there with heavy clouds. I studied the irregular mountain formations with green forests and the great stretches of plains where nomadic tribespeople grazed their cattle. For a fleeting moment I caught sight of regal Mt. Kenya, the country's highest peak. An extinct volcanic cone, Mt. Kenya with its glaciers seemed to send out a challenge to me to conquer her. Before I left Africa, I had to test my mountain-climbing ability! However, if I had the opportunity, Kilimanjaro, Africa's tallest, would be my choice, Mt. Kenya's challenge notwithstanding.

Flying in Africa takes the skill of an experienced bush pilot. The radio is of little help, and in the bush there are no smooth runways. It's strictly flying by the seat of your pants and hoping that no animal wanders into the path of the plane on landing or takeoff, or that the wheels of the landing gear don't strike a hole or some unseen object.

My eyes must have bulged as Arnie tipped the plane a bit and pointed up ahead to the right to a clearing on a mountainside.

"There she is—Gatab," Arnie said.

"This is going to be like landing on a tabletop!" I tried to force a smile. The mountain dropped off some two thousand feet into sort of a cliff at the front end of the landing strip.

"This is why we had to weigh all the contents of the plane so carefully. We don't want to miss the landing strip." Arnie explained that we would be landing slightly uphill and that the landing might be a bit rough because of irregularities in the landing strip and the possibility of gusty crosswinds. "But hold on," he said, "we've made it before and we'll make it again."

Experience put the plane down relatively smoothly. Walking toward us smiling broadly as we climbed out of the plane was veteran missionary Paul Teasdale, a rugged pioneer-type man in his thirties, one of several AIM personnel at Gatab. He drove us in his truck over a rutty, boulder-strewn road that I feared would jolt the fillings out of my teeth. The missionary compound, about a half mile from the landing strip, consists of cinder block buildings, including a small church and medical clinic operated by a nurse. The houses are simply constructed, reminding me of lakeside summer cottages I had enjoyed in the States. They have indoor plumbing, with partitions as walls but no ceilings. The house functions, though it is unfinished. "We've got too many things to do to spend the time necessary to finish the house with ceilings and woodwork," was the explanation the missionaries gave. "As long as a house is livable, that's all that matters. God's work takes time."

After having tea with Paul and Betty Lou Teasdale, Dr. Allen and I went to a cinder block building with perhaps five beds, to see patients gathered there by the nurses. The missionary nurse at Gatab, like all AIM nurses at other bush clinics, sees patients every day, treating with tender care, and weeding out those who need to be seen by a physician. If she ever has an emergency, she may radio for help. There were several cases to be seen but no major medical problems—malaria, bronchitis, parasites, and the like. One Samburu young man was recovering from tetanus. The nurse's care had been adequate in all cases, so Dr. Allen and I had little to add.

Here, as at other mission clinics, patients pay only a token fee to cover the cost of medicine and prevent multiple unnecessary visits.

Dinner with Paul and Betty Lou and others from the compound proved extremely satisfying. I reflected on how remarkable the missionary wife is, accomplishing so much without the convenience of supermarkets and automatic kitchens. Most staple foods are flown in, but most fresh foods come from the garden alongside the missionary's home. These people of Gatab reminded me of what pioneers of the United States must have been like. They are a vigorous people, with strong independent personalities that come through loud and clear. Betty Lou, the only child of veteran missionary parents, was more than typical in character and personality of what was necessary to survive in the bush of Africa. I called her "Annie Oakley"! I enjoyed these people. Our conversation around the table was brisk, lively, and fascinating. But shortly after dusk there came a lull, and eyelids grew heavy, including mine. So we called an end to the day and went to bed.

I was surprised at how quickly the sun rose, despite the early bedtime. Breakfast was over by 7 o'clock and we hopped in Paul Teasdale's Chevrolet truck for the jarring ride back to the landing strip.

If the landing at Gatab is considered exciting, the takeoff is much more so! Arnie warmed the engine a few moments, prayed, and headed toward the clifflike drop-off. In one way or another we would be airborne by the time we reached the end of the landing strip. As the plane gained speed the hillside seemed to run out from under us, and suddenly we were in the air. Then, as we flew out over the drop-off, I braced myself as a tremendous updraft shot the plane skyward, giving me the strange feeling that the seat of my pants was approaching my chin. Arnie Newman glanced at me, and assured me that all was normal and we would soon level out to a smooth flight.

Our flight to Loglogo, a station in the midst of the plains southeast of Gatab, started at approximately six thousand feet and lasted about an hour. Here the contrast to Gatab was interesting.

Loglogo was dry and desolate, with little scenery to catch the eye. The airstrip was smooth and barely visible in the midst of the dry and desolate area. Several Rendile adults and children surrounded the plane after Arnie switched off the engine.

My eye swept the inhospitable desert country and I wondered how human beings could manage to survive—let alone manage a living—in this arid land of lava rock and sparse scrub. But obviously the Rendile are of hardy stock. I learned that they follow the rains, making life a continual search for water and grazing. Camels, which provide them with milk and meat and also with transport, are their mainstay, but today they also own cattle, sheep, and goats. For the period they live in an area, they keep their livestock in an enclosure guarded by a makeshift thorn fence and their huts of animal hide and grass. When they move on to another grazing area, they dismantle the huts and carry the hides, grass matting, and poles on the backs of their camels or their wives'. The Rendile are a handsome, proud people, whose women show the family wealth by a lavish display of beads and bracelets, the latter worn both below and above the elbows. A skin or cloth wraparound completes the dress of the women and is the sole dress for the men. Married women who have borne a son wear a large coxcomb, molded from fat and ocher-colored mud.

Here at Loglogo I wondered if I might perhaps see one little Rendile boy whom I had seen briefly two years before when I was in Kenya on the medical society tour. Had he moved on with his family? He had been under the care of mission doctor Bill Barnett for bilateral clubfeet. I glanced quickly over the crowd that had gathered. I spotted my little patient fairly easily. He was the only one wearing shoes, his being the above-the-ankle shoes for clubfoot victims. Actually, the only thing he had on were the shoes! A little later, having removed his shoes, I saw that one foot had been well corrected but the other needed additional surgery. I arranged to have him flown to Kijabe, where later I corrected the problem.

The mission clinic, church, and houses are the usual cinder block variety, again finished just to the point of function. The mission nurse presented her patients—the usual variety. One young lad had severe anemia. His case would be referred to the Marsabit government hospital forty miles away for laboratory diagnosis as well as treatment.

As the sun set it became apparent that a large fire was burning to the south of the mission station. It appeared to be just a few miles away, but more trained eyes estimated the distance to be closer to twenty. Investigation revealed that a lion had killed a camel and had then retreated into the brush. The Rendile had attempted to flush out the lion by setting a small fire. However, the crosswind had spread the fire until it was out of hand. At some point it would burn itself out. There seemed to be a little danger that it would reach the mission station.

Again, as at Gatab, we dined with a missionary family, the Dilly Andersons, and others from the compound. Dilly, one of four sons of Earl and Esther Anderson, pioneer missionaries of AIM in Kenya, was a schoolmate of Paul Teasdale at RVA. Both have lived most of their lives in Africa. As we ate, the intense heat of the day subsided to a brisk, cool evening. Bedtime here, as at all outposts, was early.

At 4 A.M. I awakened to the beat of drums and strange-sounding chants. Were the Rendile on the warpath? Did they resent more white men coming into their territory? But the sounds did not seem to be approaching the mission station. I looked out my window to see if there were lights on in any of the houses of the compound. I saw no activity and decided that if the missionaries weren't concerned, neither should I be. I later learned that the Rendile were simply having a party and likely were drunk. I couldn't blame myself for being a bit frightened, having heard so many stories of people getting cooked in a pot to the beating of a drum.

Whereas Gatab and Loglogo had six to eight missionaries on duty, Ngurunit, some eighty miles west of Loglogo, had just one couple with their two-year-old son. This station is out in the midst of nowhere, the site having been selected because of its remoteness coupled with the availability of good water from the nearby mountain. Charlie Barnett, nephew of Dr. Bill Barnett, and his wife, Doris, seem to enjoy this lonely existence, with the only English-speaking people coming in by plane. Their dwelling consists of a camper-trailer with a shed that functions as a storage and toolhouse. Plumbing is nonexistent. The clinic building is, again, of cinder block. Here Charlie and Doris Barnett, though unschooled in medicine, do what they can, treating patients with loving care by dispensing medicine on a simple basis. One man had a badly broken leg, which the Barnetts had in traction. They had a variety of other cases: ulcers, osteomyelitis, polio, pneumonia. The Barnetts must transfer any unusual case to Marsabit government hospital, two hundred miles to the north. Our visit proved a bit frustrating. We realized we could do little because of the lack of facilities.

The tribespeople here are primarily Rendile, with occasional Somalis from the northeast corner of Kenya. The Somalis are statuesque people with long, slender limbs and graceful necks. Their fine facial features frequently form countenances of considerable beauty.

Arnie had flown elsewhere, so instead of flying we traveled in Charlie's truck from Ngurunit to Ilaut, about thirty miles to the north. As so often is the case in Kenya, the animals caught my eye: giraffes and elephants along with impalas and Grant gazelles. Near a riverbed we saw many prints in the soft ground, indicating to Charlie's trained eye that a pride of lions had passed that way recently. "See this track, the largest one? This is the male." Charlie stood and looked about. I surmised that if size of footprints were an indication, this was one large cat! Charlie also pointed out rhino droppings, giving further excitement to the safari. I had been assured that these great animals fear man. I hoped so. All I had was one trusty Swiss army knife, though in the cab of the truck Charlie had a rifle.

Here we were in Samburu territory. The Samburu call themselves "the world's top people." Like so many other tribes-people, they cling tenaciously to their own way of life, seeking out grazing in the semidesert lands for their humpback cattle. The war-riors are colorful characters with red-ochered pigtails, and their toughness is legendary. To avenge the death of one of his cattle, a young warrior will track down a lion and kill it with only his spear. Samburu women, like the Rendile women, love to adorn themselves with trinkets and beaded finery. And like so many other tribes, the Samburu make tribal ceremonies the center of their lives, starting with initiation in early years.

I noted that the riverbed at Ilaut was absolutely dry, yet here were the Samburu. If they needed water, why on earth were they here? Then I observed that they obtain water by digging into the sand. Three men at different levels of the pit lift the water with a grunting cadence, one handing the bucket of water to the other. I watched them water their camels. The animals looked dry and shrunken, but after consuming perhaps up to forty gallons of water they appeared suddenly fat and full. It was an amazing sight to see. The water must move quickly from their cardiovascular tree into the interstitial tissues. Otherwise the animal would collapse from water intoxication.

The clinic at Ilaut was held under a large acacia tree, with Charlie's truck serving as a pharmacy and the great outdoors as the examining room. While the clinic was being conducted, a tape recorder played Bible stories in the Samburu tongue. The children as well as the adults were fascinated by the "box that talks." If the recorded voice asked, "Are you lonely?" or some other question, the listeners would answer. I was told that some people are, of course, simply curious—as I observed—but occasionally children or adults will give the impression that they are truly listening to the Word of God.

The local interpreter was a dynamic man dressed in a western shirt with a colorful checkered skirt rather than trousers. He inter-preted from Swahili into the Samburu language. Dr. Allen and I easily cared for the first woman and her two children. But, strange-ly, the woman did not leave as I examined the next two women, number two with four children and number three with two children. One of the two children had a bowel problem and we administered a tablespoonful of milk of magnesia. He promptly spit it out, causing our interpreter to react rather vigorously. He grasped the boy firmly and scolded in words I could not understand, but I was pretty sure it was something like, "The man is going to give you another spoonful of medicine. This time swallow it or else!" The second tablespoonful of medicine disappeared with a gulp.

After numbers two and three left with the children, the first woman lingered as a fourth woman appeared, this one much younger and quite attractive. She had no children. Hers was a minor complaint—a cold, I think—and as she left, the older woman went with her. Suddenly I caught on and said,"Hey, is that your family?"

Our interpreter beamed proudly. "Yes, my wives and my children." The older woman was his first wife, and the fourth obviously his youngest, sort of a playmate, probably selected by wife number one, who obviously was in charge of the household. Questioning the man further, I learned that all four wives live in the same area, but not in the same hut. I wanted to take a family picture, but the husband politely but firmly refused.

Returning to Ngurunit was even more exciting than our trip down, since dusk had slipped up on us. Should we have car trouble, this could prove to be a very interesting place to camp. Happily, no problems developed, and we pulled up just in time for dinner. These missionary women continued to amaze me with their ability to cope with difficult situations. On this particular occasion, I felt as though I were part of the cast of a Western movie. Doris Barnett cooked over an open fire, and we sat there eating tasty victuals, licking our fingers, just like on the old "Wagon Train" shows.

Early bedtime gave me the choice of sleeping in the storage area on a cot or moving the cot outdoors beneath mosquito netting slung between two chairs. I elected to sleep outdoors, feeling that the magnificent starry sky would be quite an experience. This experience lasted about two minutes before deep sleep left me un-conscious till morning. I could not remember sleeping so soundly, ever. This was certainly a great way to live!

Rising to the sound of cracking wood, I tensed as I saw not more than two hundred yards away three elephants munching their way through the brush, having breakfast. Their munching consisted of ripping down tree branches. The grass and other vegetation was so dry that the elephants were now literally destroying the forest. Charlie and I walked over within fifty yards of these huge beasts but didn't move any closer. Again I realized how powerless I was, my total armament being my Swiss army knife!

At breakfast one of the African workers reported rhino tracks near camp, which apparently had been made during the night. This "great white hunter" managed to sleep through not only the dazzling beauty of the starry sky but also a rhino visit and would have missed the elephants had it not been for their noisy eating.

We flew to another clinic at Kalacha, the newest AIM station in the eastern NFD. Here we encountered people of the Boran tribe, who had a reputation for being unusually fierce. Paul Teasdale told us that tribal outbursts between the Boran and Rendile were gruesome. Paul had made original contact with the Boran and had encountered no problems, other than that they actually turned their backs on him when he tried to present the Gospel of Christ to them. They are Satan worshipers.

The clinic, again, was held outdoors under an acacia tree. The Boran flocked in to see the nurse and physicians, some out of curiosity, others because of pathological difficulties. Gonorrhea is a major problem, since the men tend to sleep around a great deal. They have sort of a "new morality" code—the kind that sex magazines in the United States advocate as being "enlightened liv-ing." Here at Kalacha I treated two men for gonorrhea—one was seventy-six, the other ninety-nine! These ages are estimated by relating the patient's life to known events in the history of Kenya or the life of President Kenyatta.

It was encouraging to learn that a permanent dispensary would later be constructed. A Christian government "dresser," it was hoped, would operate the clinic. I wondered if a missionary and his family could survive in such a desolate place as Kalacha. But I wouldn't be too sure. The patience and diligence and ability to adapt to rugged conditions on the part of these missionaries absolutely amazed me. Certainly they had to have a sense of God's calling them to this work in order to continue to serve these people under such circumstances.

Our flight back to Gatab from Kalacha was uneventful, except for landing. As Arnie Newman approached the tabletop airstrip, we observed cattle sauntering across the landing area. I held on as he buzzed the herd, unsuccessfully. Crossing the updraft, however, at the end of the airstrip, proved even more exciting, for suddenly we were shooting upward at a speed greater than that of any roller coaster. Even more than when we took off from Gatab, I had that sickening sensation that my shoulders would slide right out through my seat, and my stomach seemed to be up between my ears. Needless to say, I was most happy when, after two additional buzzings, the cattle finally cleared and we touched down.

Again our evening with Paul and Betty Lou Teasdale was a delightful experience as we swapped stories and spoke of God's care. We ran into one slight problem: only one bathroom for the Teasdales, a couple visiting from Lincoln, Nebraska, Dr. Allen, and myself. Paul commented with a shrug, "The great outdoors is adequate for the menfolk."

Before retiring for the night Dr. Allen, dressed in pajamas exposing spindly legs between the short pants and his shoetops, said in his Australian drawl, "Well, I will, in fact, use the great outdoors."

A few moments later, my scrawny companion returned, his hair windblown and a note of disgust written on his face. "The great outdoors is all well and good for the menfolk," he drawled, "but Paul did not mention those two friendly hounds. They kept bashing into me. It was frightfully difficult to get the job done under such circumstances!"

On awaking at sunrise, I caught sight of Dr. John's windblown hair in the next bunk. I burst out laughing, thinking about the "great outdoors" and those "friendly hounds."

Since the Teasdales had business at Nairobi, they had made plans to take the visiting couple, a nurse, Dr. Allen, and me back to the medical center—home, in my case. This would give me a feel for Africa as I traveled by road for two days. We left Gatab in a truck and a station wagon, both with four-wheel drive, necessary for travel on rugged African roads. We rode the first two hours down a torturous bumpy road from the mountainside to the plains, a road handbuilt some years before by Paul Teasdale and other missionaries. At times it seemed the truck in which I was riding was just inches from the edge of the precipices. The magnificent beauty of the area, including sparkling Lake Rudolf and the rugged mountain scenery, left me spellbound.

On the plains the road smoothed out, and Paul Teasdale tramped heavily on the accelerator. A hot breeze played about us, in contrast to the cool winds we had experienced at Gatab. At one point we pulled over to enjoy a lunch that Betty Lou had packed. The villages we passed through were tiny, home to curious but friendly Africans from whom we could buy bracelets, necklaces, spears, and knives.

Paul had in mind camping about midpoint in our journey, but in late afternoon a broken leaf of a rear spring caused us to set up early camp in what Paul described as lion country. I was glad that I still carried my Swiss army knife.

Out of Paul's truck came all the equipment necessary to repair the broken spring, including a welding machine. In less than an hour the station wagon was roadworthy. I marveled again at the ability of this man to meet problems as they arose. It's really part of survival for the bush missionary.

After an early breakfast, we rode on toward Kijabe, passing through plains, mountains, and desert. In more plush areas we saw herds of giraffes and zebras. We ran onto the remains of a poached elephant, his tusks removed, but saw no live elephant. It was an exciting but uneventful day, except for a flat tire. The irregularity of the meals gnawed at my stomach but seemed to have no effect on the missionaries.

My family greeted me with great enthusiasm and warmth, though some held their noses. I, of course, hadn't seen a bathtub since I left. "Whew, daddy, do you ever stink! You look like a Skid Row bum." The children, however, stepped back to look admiringly at my eight-day beard. "Why don't you keep it, daddy!" squealed Krissy. "It makes you look so cute." Janet stood scowling. She had barely been able to stand the prickly kiss I gave her. "Honey, shave it off immediately, or else!" Around the table I had many tales to tell, along with trinkets to pass out to each family member. The children, from the oldest down to the youngest, seemed genuinely interested, and there was no fidgeting or walking away from the table as is sometimes the case when I try to share.

In addition to stories of tribespeople I had treated, I spoke of the remarkable missionaries I had met. Their ability to adapt to primitive conditions that most of us wouldn't be able to take impressed me. The bush missionaries spend a great deal of time just simply existing. They must maintain all of their equipment and transportation as well as provide their daily bread. The patience and diligence of these people in meeting with the Africans for morning and evening prayer showed a faithfulness of great degree. With perhaps only two or three non-Christians present in such a gathering, missionaries will make it a point to present the Gospel on a very elementary level, pointing out that God loves humans so much that he will forgive their sin and take them into his family wholly through the merits of his only Son, Jesus Christ. They firmly believe and proclaim the words of Jesus, "I am the way, the truth, and the life: no man cometh unto the Father, but by Me" (John 14:6).

At home in our churches we should realize that the bush missionary is a different breed. He or she is used to simple presentations. When we ask him or her to stand before a large congregation or even a Sunday school class to preach a message of depth in English, this must be an extremely frustrating experience. We need to learn to accept them as they are—unsophisticated, faithful servants of God from the bush.

6

Tanzanian Safari

In early October I purchased a sparkling new white, red-trimmed Kombi, a combination car-bus with three rows of seats that would comfortably accommodate our family of eleven only because three were little people. Having been exposed sufficiently to African roads on the Northern Frontier safari, I itched to test the Kombi on a trip with the family. Our chance came in late October. Rift Valley Academy closed for a long weekend, a quarterly procedure designed to send missionary kids (MKs) home to their parents for a visit. Would Janet, as a member of the faculty, help chaperon a busload going to Tanzania? The answer was an enthusiastic yes, since she would be permitted to take seven of our children aboard the bus and I could drive the Kombi with our other two kids and follow along. For me it would be almost totally nonmedical, giving me a chance to see more of Africa and be with members of my family.

This trip into Tanzania suggested adventure from the start. Apprehension spread among the students who were going with us. Rumors had it that the People's Militia of Tanzania had in some cases harrassed travelers as they crossed the border. It seemed they were uptight over certain styles. In Tanzania, once-topless African women now were required by law to cover up. So the border guards were making it rough on tourists and others who, in their opinion, dressed immodestly. In one incident, two women reportedly were mortified when a guard took exception to their short skirts and ripped them off. The People's Militia also, word had it, disliked males with tight-fitting pants and long hair. And there could be no items made of the skin of African animals—not even a watchband.

So the Tanzania-bound MKs scurried about to conform. The girls who did not have ankle-length skirts either borrowed them or made sort of a sarong for themselves out of yard goods. The test for pants was simple: if a boy could pass a Coke bottle down the leg, his pants were OK; otherwise he borrowed an oversized pair, possibly from an adult. The sound of clippers in action completed the preparation as boy after boy appeared with rather nonprofessional haircuts.

Some sixty of these rather odd-looking students piled into a bus, along with Janet and seven of our kids. Debbie, Paul, and I followed in the Kombi. I had spent two days in Nairobi getting a temporary Tanzanian license for the Kombi as well as visas for our family. It is unbelievable how much time one must take in Africa to care for details. However, these developing nations have a great deal of national pride. They want their regulations followed by everyone. I did not find that unreasonable.

Driving to the border of Tanzania took us past the Amboseli Game Reserve, a dramatically scenic twelve-hundred-square-mile area just north of Kilimanjaro. On the bus, according to Janet, fourteen young Jorden eyes almost popped from their sockets as we passed buffalo, elephants, giraffes, zebras, and many varieties of antelope. I drove in fear of striking one of these animals, for they seemed oblivious to the passing traffic. But we passed through without incident.

Now we faced the ordeal of crossing the border. On board the bus Janet and students prayed that there would be no problems.

But fear gripped the young people. "What if a guard frisks me and gets fresh?" "What if they don't like the way someone is dressed?" "What if they take something away from us?" The answer to each question was the same: "You can do nothing about it. Just don't worry."

Happily, things went smoothly. It took about an hour for the border guards to check passports and other papers, but there was no frisking or other unpleasant incidents. Our precautionary measures had been right, and God had answered prayer. As we traveled on into Tanzania, a police barricade stopped us and checked the bus, but no problems developed.

Aboard the bus Janet learned the meaning of the term "bush stop." A couple of the students asked her after we had been traveling for several hours, "Is it all right if we ask the driver to stop for a bush stop?"

Uninitiated but not wanting the students to know, Janet responded, "Do you usually make bush stops? If so, all right." It sounded like fun.

The students talked to the African driver, and presently he stopped the bus off the road. All the students piled out, and Janet suddenly realized the meaning of the term. The girls went on one side of the road behind the bushes, while the boys went on the other side, lined up behind the bushes, their backs to the road. There are no Texaco or Standard stations, no oases with rest room facilities on these African roads. If you must go, it must be in the great outdoors. Slowly Janet eased out of her seat and headed for the door, just like a veteran missionary.

Tanzania didn't appear a great deal different from Kenya, though it was hot and uncomfortable compared to what we had been used to in the higher elevations of the Kijabe region. The Great Rift Valley extends through Tanzania, with the land rising to plateaus about four thousand feet above sea level westward from the coast. Much of the area is hot, dry grasslands with an occasional thorn tree, in some respects a lot like plains of the Southwest in the United States.

Surgeon on Safari

Towering out of this area in northern Tanzania, just to the east of where we crossed the border, is majestic, snowcapped Kilimanjaro, loftiest peak in all of Africa. We had glimpsed her from the Amboseli Game Reserve, and now from Arusha, some sixty miles south into Tanzania, we could see more of the great mountain. Someday I'd try to climb Kilimanjaro, but not on this particular trip.

In Arusha, a small city where the last of our RVA students were dropped off for their visits with their parents, we met a different breed of missionary. Salaried by large denominations, they work in Bible schools and seminaries and hold administrative jobs. Their homes are adequate, are furnished pleasantly, and give the impression of a bit of America in Tanzania. These are not bush missionaries, nor do they pretend to be. They are quick to say that they do not make the sacrifices of the bush missionary. Their main sacrifice is being away from their families. But this in itself is something, I decided, when one considers the excitement of having college kids home for the holidays, or married kids who, with their children, visit grandpa and grandma periodically.

The salaried missionary does not have a great deal of concern for the financial side of life. The mission may own his house and automobile and may even maintain them. Certainly the Lord has selected different types of personalities for the mission field. Those who enjoy totally relying on God for their supplies are usually back in the bush; others function better under the conditions we saw in Arusha.

But both kinds of missionaries are needed when the total job of missions is considered. God needs people who fit into the various positions. A football team consists of running backs, quarterbacks, tight ends, linemen, to name a few, all with mental and physical attributes that are suited for their jobs. The missionary team seems to be similar. Just as there are advantages and disadvantages in playing a certain position on a football team, so it is with the missionary team. As I considered this, I realized that God can use all of these personalities with their special talents. I determined not to

72

think more highly of one type of missionary than another. The missionary doctor is no more important than the bush missionary, and the bush missionary is no greater in God's eyes than the faithful missionary executive or office clerk.

After much discussion as to what we should do on Sunday, we decided to worship God on the move rather than stay in Arusha for church. We decided to leave early for a place that had been described to us as not unlike a Garden of Eden—the Ngorongoro Crater. We would worship God in the quietness of our hearts in this magnificent setting. God would understand. He is not confined to church buildings.

We were up and on our way shortly after 5 A.M., after dressing quietly and slipping out without awakening our host and hostess. It was pitch dark, and the Tarmac road leading out of Arusha was deserted. Our Kombi was loaded down with our family of eleven, along with water and food for lunch. I only hoped we didn't have any sort of mechanical breakdown. I quietly committed the matter to my heavenly Father.

Our drive was a little less than a hundred miles, but the road was in such poor condition that it was nearly nine o'clock before Ngorongoro loomed in the distance. At 10,165 feet, it is one of six of Africa's 10,000-foot mountains clustered in a hundred square mile game sanctuary. In the area Masai herd their cattle and goats, sharing the land with the wild game.

In order to enter the crater, we discovered that we had to hire a guide and a four-wheel drive Land Rover at a cost of fifty dollars. The cost was more than we had expected, but to make matters worse our family required two Land Rovers. Fortunately, a young couple and a friend who were squirming at the high cost chipped in and joined us. Janet and I considered putting all the small kids in with our three new acquaintances. But somehow this doesn't seem fair—nor Christian.

As we rode along the rim, we saw immediately why Ngorongoro is considered one of the world's marvels. Here in this vast caldera lies a hidden world of Edenlike plains, hills, and forest. Said to have the greatest permanent concentration of wildlife in Africa, this national park is a paradise for wildebeests, zebras, gazelles, and other plains animals. But it ceases to be a true Garden of Eden for many of these animals when packs of hyenas attack. Even old or crippled lions may fall victim to the bold ferocity of a pack of hyenas, which are generally considered to be just scavengers, finishing up kills of larger animals. Besides lions, there are two other species of the big five: rhinos and buffalo. But it is the pride of lions that attracts the most attention. Safari vehicles can drive rather close to them as they sprawl lazily in the grass, unperturbed, partly because they're used to visitors and partly because the car fumes seem to cover human odors.

At one area we watched a male lion with his kingly mane and his mate make love. The male sat beside the lioness, gazing off into the distance with a rather majestic, arrogant expression. The lioness seemed as indifferent to him as she did to the tourists with their clicking cameras. Even during copulation, her attitude remained one of total indifference. At orgasm he bit into the back of her neck in a loving manner. She responded by rolling over on her back to playfully paw at his cheeck. This was her only response to his attentions. Again he resumed the arrogant gaze into the distance as she promptly fell asleep.

This observation caused me to chuckle. The arrogant gaze of the male lion somehow reminded me so much of certain human males who have complained about their spouses' indifference to their romantic interests. Possibly they are too much like the king of beasts!

None of our family seemed to be embarrassed by this episode. Family communication has always been free and natural in regard to sex education in our home. We have learned to speak about parts of the human body by using their correct names. Our children have felt free to come home from school and ask, "What does———mean?"—referring to some gutter term. We have been able to discuss these terms, substituting proper terminology. We have encouraged the mating of pets, such as cats and hamsters, for educational purposes. On one occasion, Krissy reported, "My male hamster is dumb. He doesn't even know how to mate. He gets up on her head!"

Our return trip to Arusha took us through the Lake Manyara game preserve, a 123-square mile national park stretching along the western shore of Lake Manyara. Its glades, swamps, savannah, and dense forest are alive with a wide variety of game. The park's most famous attractions are tree-climbing lions, who apparently took to trees to escape the numerous buffalo. Or maybe they wanted a better look at the yellow and olive baboons or the blue-and black-faced vervet monkeys. Bird lovers pause long at the lake shore to watch pelicans, spoonbills, flamingos, and many other species. Here, as in other parts of Africa, elephants have right of way. So we didn't argue when a herd of elephants passed directly in front of our Kombi, bringing us to a sudden stop. Janet edged close to me and hardly dared breathe, but the kids watched with great delight. When we finally arrived back in Arusha at 7:30 that evening, we were an exhausted family but agreed that we'd had one of the greatest days of our lives. We thanked God for allowing us to see so many wonders of his great creation and added another thanks for giving us safe travel over some almost impossible roads.

On Monday I was all in favor of going to another game park. However, my children wanted to go swimming at one of the hotels. Somehow it seemed ridiculous to spend time swimming, something we could do in the States, when we could be seeing more of these marvelous African animals. But I felt we should do what the kids wanted to do, so I reluctantly drove them out to the pool.

Here, as God would have it, we met a man who gave me valuable counsel concerning the trip that Paul, Debbie, and I planned to take. Janet and the other children were returning to Kijabe with the RVA students, and I would drive the Kombi on an extended trip through northwestern Tanzania. Elder Jackson, a Southern Baptist missionary, was in Arusha with his family; his daughters were students at RVA, and we enjoyed meeting their parents. As we talked about our trip, I learned that I had badly misjudged the driving time from Arusha to Shinyanga. Instead of an eight-hour drive, Mr. Jackson said it would be closer to twenty hours, mostly due to road conditions. He invited us to stop at their mission station at Kiomboi, the midpoint en route to Shinyanga. I accepted gladly, thankful to know the facts concerning the trip. Tanzania is not as developed as Kenya, and there are few stores for purchasing suitable food along the highways. We could easily have been caught without adequate food and water. Here was a case of God's protecting the innocent—or was it the ignorant?

After bidding Janet and the other children good-bye, Debbie, Paul, and I headed west. Despite the fact the map indicated a red-line highway, I realized some red lines mean minor roads. For mile after mile our road was a nightmare of holes, boulders, and irregularities. We found ourselves averaging less than fifteen miles an hour. Indeed, there was no way we could have made Shinyanga in one day.

We arrived at Kiomboi in late afternoon. Mr. Jackson, who operates a Bible school for Africans, was on the playground teaching students how to play softball. Paul and I volunteered to play with them. After the rules had been explained to the Africans, teams were chosen. I was disappointed to be among the last chosen. Apparently I looked older than I thought. Again my pride suffered when the batting order placed me near the bottom. Was I some kind of tottering old man?

The first few African batters had great difficulty making contact with the ball. Yet my attempts to coach them met with coolness. Again, this disturbed my male ego.

Finally, my turn at bat arrived. The first pitch to me was right across the middle of the plate. Keeping my eye carefully on the ball, I swung. The ball soared far over the heads of the outfielders, and I casually loped around the bases for a home run. Interestingly, my teammates suddenly became attentive to my coaching. My day had been made.

Dinner with the Jacksons proved a pleasant experience. We talked about mission work and raising a family on the mission field. Their grown son, Noel, felt that going to a boarding school was not a bad idea for a teen-ager. "It gives the teen-ager opportunity to be with his peers for three months and then with his family one month," he explained. "The teen years are a time when peers are really important, so the proportion of time seems about right."

His parents explained that they made a point to make that month he spent with them truly a family time. They were reluctant to let their work interfere with their children. I concluded that this may be the key to raising children on the mission field. Some missionaries I knew had not discovered this key, letting their work take precedence to the disadvantage of their children.

Next morning a bright African sun awoke us for an early breakfast. "There's a long stretch of desert you'll want to cross before noon," Mrs. Jackson said as she hurried to get us off. Again it appeared that God was intervening on our behalf, protecting the innocent.

Driving through the desert was an experience I'll long remember. I kept wondering what might happen if we had car trouble. The Kombi seemed like a metal oven. Debbie and Paul casually slept while I drove along the corrugated, difficult road. I must have prayed well over an hour as I drove along. For some unknown reason I did not feel in complete control of the situation. There were few people to be seen anywhere. Occasionally a truck or a large bus would all but crowd us off the road. On one occasion Debbie commented on a close brush with a bus that came barreling at us down the middle of the road. "Honey," I said, "give me a Sherman tank for Christmas and we'll return to Tanzania and get even with these trucks and buses!" I continued to pray as I drove, wondering what men do who don't know God.

Arriving in Shinyanga in late afternoon, we found Norm Dilworth, an AIM missionary. Norm and Sheila, with their two young sons, had been in Shinyanga for a year, having served earlier at Kijabe. Norm gave me the impression that he was happy wherever the Lord wanted him, and I judged that here was a man who could serve equally well as either a bush or urban missionary.

Norm was anxious for us to meet his local African pastor, so we climbed back into the Kombi and drove to the other side of town. We visited with this gracious black man, whom I estimated to be about fifty, out front of his conventional mud hut with a thatched roof. I learned that he has ten children, three of whom are university graduates. All of his children were in school. I marveled at this man living in the simplest of circumstances having such a progressive attitude. God, I realized, was choosing his leaders carefully to draw out those who would become the people of God here in Tanzania.

That evening we had a pleasant dinner with the Dilworths, again talking about God's work as well as the rearing of children on the mission field. Then we pored over my road map, discussing how to get to Mwanza on the southern shores of Lake Victoria to visit Darwin and Carolyn Dunham, a couple of Wheatonites serving under AIM in the mission's literature ministry. Darwin is a super artist.

Next morning we set out with Norm in his Toyota Land Cruiser to visit the mission hospital at Kola Ndoto, a few miles north of Shinyanga. I noted that his Land Cruiser took the corrugated roads much better than our Kombi. After meeting some of the staff and touring the hospital, I surmised that Africans were receiving excellent treatment. But the hospital was woefully short of physicians, and there wasn't an orthopedic surgeon anywhere in the entire area. A visit to the company hospital at the diamond mine topped off the day.

Next morning Norm sent us on our way to Mwanza from a prone position. His small son Johnnie, I had noticed the day before, had a cold, and Norm had shared a soft drink with the boy. Anytime an adult catches a virus from a child, look out—the adult probably will be markedly more ill. Norm planned on spending the next day or so in bed.

Only a few miles outside Shinyanga it became apparent that something was amiss with the Kombi. I could hear a firm cracking noise directly under the driver's seat as we hit the ridges in the road. We limped into Kola Ndoto, hoping to find a mechanic. The only mechanic in town was away, but an apprentice said he could do work that would get us back to Shinyanga. In addition to a broken shock absorber, it was apparent that two of the four bolts of the right front wheel suspension had been sheared and the other two bolts had come loose from the chassis. Apparently the drive through the desert had taken its toll. I remembered then how hard I'd prayed. God had gotten us to our destination on two suspension bolts rather than four!

While the apprentice worked on the car, we visited with Mrs. Maynard, a vigorous, unpretentious nurse at the mission hospital who had served in Africa for thirty-five years. She loaned us her Land Rover and provided lunch for Debbie, Paul, and me. There was a gracious sternness about her, evidenced by her gentle but firm remark to teen-age Paul as he politely refused second or third servings, "I do not like leftovers." Paul happily obliged. Teen-aged boys must have hollow legs.

Later, when we returned to Shinyanga, Norm Dilworth, though ill, got up to go with me to a local Asian auto parts shop. A mechanic replaced the broken shock absorber with one that was an inch too short, along with homemade suspension bolts to secure the right front wheel enough to—we hoped—get us to Mwanza, where there was an authorized Volkswagen dealer.

Following an early supper, we headed prayerfully for Mwanza, driving through the African night over the washboard road. The Dunhams had been expecting us all day but were not surprised at our late arrival at 11:30. "This type of thing happens all the time in Africa," Darwin commented. I expressed my concern for the Kombi, only to learn that the next day was a national holiday so the garages would likely be closed. We chatted for a while then decided that a good night's rest was the best solution for the moment.

Fortunately next day we found an Asian garage, where the mechanic not only seemed knowledgeable about Volkswagens but actually had four much needed heavy-duty shocks for a Kombi. That was good news; the bad news was the work would cost $190 and I had only $200. We needed money for gasoline, as well as for food and lodging to make our way back to Kijabe. But we couldn't make it back without reliable wheels. So the work was done and paid for. I'm sure Darwin would have come to my rescue with funds had I shared my predicament, but missionaries must live by faith. I was a missionary. So we would trust God to get us home despite my flat wallet.

After getting clear instructions for passing through the Serengeti Plains and the Serengeti National Park, we said good-bye to the Dunhams and headed north toward Kijabe. Here again we stared wide-eyed at herds of buffalo, giraffes, impalas, and wildebeests. In late afternoon, we stopped at the Seronera Lodge but found it closed. And no gasoline was available. It was already sunset, and Tanzanian regulations forbade our traveling through a game park at night. A ranger directed us to Lobo Lodge, an hour and a half away.

The lodge was jam-packed. But that was of little concern—we didn't have enough money for lodging. We bought dinner with our diminishing money, setting aside the rest for one more meal and a fill-up for the Kombi. We slept in the Kombi in the parking lot of the lodge. It was fun—well, at least different.

Leaving the Serengeti, we arrived at the Kenyan border. I tried to change my Tanzanian shillings, all I had in money, into Kenyan shillings but got only shrugs of the shoulder. We would go wholly on faith the rest of the way. Driving through the Masai Mara Game Reserve just across the border, we slowed to watch a pride of lions.

They had made a kill and were feasting just off the road. "If our gas doesn't hold out, *we* could end up being a feast," I quipped.

But we arrived back at Kijabe with gasoline to spare. We were exhausted, hungry, and broke except for our Tanzanian shillings. God had supplied all our needs. We felt a little like real faith missionaries.

7
Kilimanjaro:
"House of God"

Kilimanjaro, the king of African mountains, rises like a jewel from the flat plains of northern Tanzania, her snowcapped western peak, Kibo, etched against the blue sky on clear days. Masai tribesmen who herd their cattle in the shadow of the great mountain speak of the summit as *Ngàje Ngài*, "The House of God." Ernest Hemingway popularized this legendary idea in his famous short story "The Snows of Kilimanjaro."

We saw Kilimanjaro on several occasions. I'll never forget our vacation in Amboseli Game Reserve. The great mountain was only twenty-five miles away, but being fickle, Kili hid from us behind a cloud cover. As we were having morning devotions, my family suddenly stampeded past me with their cameras. I turned and saw Kilimanjaro towering before me in all her glory. The cloud cover had suddenly vanished. Cameras clicked, and our family gazed in awe at the magnificent mountain. Then, mysteriously, Kili disappeared as suddenly as it had appeared. God, I'm sure, winked at the sudden interruption of our devotional time. You've got to be quick for Kili!

I got my chance to conquer Kilimanjaro on another occasion. RVA's ecology class, along with our Debbie and Paul, elected to take a five-day trip to Kili's 19,340-foot summit, Kibo. Beth and two other biology students joined the group, making about twenty RVAers in all. Healthy, able-bodied chaperons were needed, and I was one of seven who volunteered. Another was Dr. Bethea.

Our little Krissy cried as we piled into our Kombi. Beth noted that fact in her diary, adding, "What a nut. I love her lots." Besides myself, there were seven others aboard—Beth, Debbie, Paul, Paul's Wheaton friend Steve Ross (who had come over for a few months), Bruce Marshall, and two other RVA students. We left Kijabe on Wednesday afternoon, January 30, along with two other carloads, and we arrived in Moshi, Tanzania, at the foot of Kilimanjaro, at 2 A.M. Thursday. Here arrangements had been made to camp in tents in the front yard of the home of a missionary couple. Following a light meal, we piled into sleeping bags on cots and got five hours' sleep. The strain of ten hours' driving at night on African roads made me extremely appreciative of the rest.

After breakfast, our group left for the hotel, where arrangements had been made for us to obtain a guide and about a dozen porters. The porters took our food and airline bags, crammed with extra clothing, leaving us unencumbered for our long climb.

Our long line of climbers, followed by the porters balancing their loads of about thirty pounds on their heads, began the challenge of Kili shortly after noon. The first day we planned to hike to mountain climbers hut no. 1, a distance of about ten miles over rough terrain. We arrived in late afternoon, a tired, hungry group of kids and chaperons. We had been in too much of a hurry to have lunch, so our supper of soup, sandwiches, and hardboiled eggs hit the spot.

After a good night's rest on wooden bunks, we arose early for a breakfast of oatmeal then had a brief time of devotions, followed by instructions concerning our hike to the second hut. Since we were now at 9,000 feet and going on to 12,300 feet, we wore heavier clothing for the twelve-mile hike. We began our second day hiking through a rain forest that was mossy, dark, and damp. An hour or so later we burst into sunlit rolling fields. And there looming above us were Kili's two peaks, Kibo and Mwanza.

"Beautiful!" "Fantastic!" "Really neat!" The magnificent sight of snowcapped Kibo and the not as tall bald Mwanza sent adrenalin into teen-agers and chaperons alike. Our mood was greatly lifted, and our stride noticeably increased. Here was an obvious spiritual lesson. Certainly if life has a purpose that we keep before us we are stimulated in what otherwise seems to be a long, slow, tedious life. Hebrews 12:1-2 says it this way for the Christian: "Let us lay aside every weight and the sin which doth so easily beset us, looking unto Jesus the author and finisher of our faith."

The higher elevations presented brilliant scenery consisting of many varieties of flowers, shrubs, and rocks. The students observed these items carefully, taking notes for their reports. I walked along with Beth and Debbie, periodically taking Beth's pulse and respiration for her report. Her pulse was almost double the normal rate of eighty. It was interesting to note that my pulse stayed lower than hers or Debbie's. We had been instructed to walk slowly, taking short strides. I found, however, that I tended to take long strides, with bursts of speed necessitating rest for longer periods. My two teen-age daughters walked along slowly and soon caught up with me at each rest stop. It reminded me of the tortoise and the hare.

Walking up Kili proved to be a rather boring activity to me in some respects. Despite the fascinating scenery, I, like the other hikers, had to keep a close eye on where I was stepping for fear of twisting an ankle. The muscles of my legs began to show signs of soreness. But after a time the pain left. Others experienced the same phenomenon. It was like a distance runner's second wind.

In late afternoon we arrived at hut no. 2, tired, hungry, and anxious for shelter from the cold winds. The temperature here at 12,300 feet was well below freezing, and the wind chill factor probably below zero. After a supper of soup, biscuits, and tea, we took time to read from the Bible and pray, and we sang quite vigorously for a group who had now walked more than twenty miles up the side of Kili. Despite the fact that hut no. 2 had no mattresses on the bunks, I slept rather soundly for a few hours. Many of the kids didn't get much sleep because of the cold.

All of our clothes were now necessary for our walk up to the third hut, which is at 15,500 feet. Again we faced cold winds and another ten-mile hike. We would cross the saddle between the two peaks of Kili.

In preparation for our climb, I had read two books on mountain climbing, noting espeically the symptoms of mountain sickness. I had been keeping a watchful eye on the students assigned to me. Beth was now starting to show definite signs of becoming ill. Yet, as a physician, I reasoned that a great deal of the sense of ill-being might be associated with the poor sleep, inadequate food, and walking up hill into the icy wind. All of this seemed to be more than a satisfactory explanation for the GI distress, headaches, and sense of weakness that seemed to be tugging at Beth and others.

As we stumbled across the saddle, a windswept, barren area reminding me of the surface of the moon, I found Jim, one of our RVA students, lying prostrate. His lips were blue, and he was experiencing difficulty in breathing. Though he was a strong young man, porters and other climbers took turns helping him the last mile to hut no. 3. I considered sending Jim back down to the second hut, but who would go with him? Perhaps he would feel better after a night's rest.

Debbie now had blisters and walked with considerable difficulty. Like Beth, she had a headache and an upset stomach. Yet I was proud of these two girls, who reached hut no. 3 by sheer courage. Much to the surprise of the girls, dear old dad was doing well. I had only a touch of a headache and no shortness of breath. My stomach was rather tender, but again I felt that this was due more to lack of enough food than to true mountain sickness.

I stood in absolute awe there at 15,500 feet, drinking in the magnificent view. A snowstorm that had temporarily blocked out the summit had subsided. Now the peak of Kilimanjaro loomed another 4,000 feet above us, its snow cone outlined against brilliant blue. Thoughts of God's greatness flooded my mind: I belong to the God who created this magnificent mountain. (What a thought!) He also created each of us, and we are made in his image.

85

The Creator-God, who knows the beginning from the end, but who knows his children so well that he knows the number of hairs on their heads. We are "pearls of great price"—for God so loved that he gave his only Son. Sometimes I think that most Christians do not recognize the value of the human being in the eyes of God. We properly emphasize the sinfulness of man, but the love of God for his creation is very apparent. At least it was to me as I stood on Kilimanjaro that late afternoon.

Again we had soup and tea for dinner and then elected to try to sleep. We would arise at 1 A.M. to conserve time and get relief from the sun, which was getting to us. However, sleep would not come; it was simply too cold, despite the fact that I wore all my clothes and was in a heavy sleeping bag. All of the group thrashed about in their beds, obviously as uncomfortable as I was.

There was no problem getting everyone up at 1 A.M. After a quick breakfast of oatmeal and tea, we prepared to leave for the climb to the peak. Other than having extremely cold toes, I felt up to the challenge of going the final three miles to the summit, to stand triumphantly on top of Kibo. It was pitch black. Except for occasional falling stars, our only light was a lantern carried by our guide.

Paul and Steve Ross went on ahead with a group that seemed a little more hardy than my group of teen-agers. I could see their forms now and then as my own hikers courageously plodded their way upward. Toes and fingers quickly numbed. Because of the lack of oxygen, we fought to satisfy our lungs. A few began talking of turning back. Somehow I had forced myself not to think of turning back, since I wanted so desperately to go all the way. After about a mile I sensed that I had at least one daughter, Beth, who probably wasn't going to be able to continue. Her warm forehead indicated a fever, and she was shaking from a chill. "My head is pounding unmercifully," she admitted. "And my stomach has never felt worse. I hate to spoil it for you and the others." She was on the verge of tears.

Deb probably could have gone farther, but she admitted that she too was not feeling well. Jim, the boy we had helped the last mile to hut no. 3 the day before, seemed to be holding his own, but I felt he would not make it much farther.

"Kids, I think we should turn back to hut no. 3. I'm as disappointed as you are, but we could have some serious problems if we push ahead." This was joyous news to Beth, as well as to Deb and Jim. Two others joined us, kids I hadn't realized were probably feeling as bad as my daughters and Jim.

After tucking my five patients into bed back in hut no. 3, using all of the extra sleeping bags to warm them up, I tried to get some sleep myself. However, Jim, sleeping in the bunk below me, kept coughing, sometimes violently; and he appeared to be lapsing into delirium. I feared that this young man was on the verge of pneumonia. I got some rest but no sleep.

At the crack of dawn I awakened my five charges and suggested that we start down the mountain for Jim's sake. I met with no resistance whatsoever. We left without breakfast, looking back frequently at the trail leading to the summit. With binoculars, we could barely make out a line of climbers slowly ascending. Again my heart was filled with keen disappointment, yet I felt that a prayerful decision had been made.

My charges and I descended following rest at the cabin. At about fourteen thousand feet it became quite apparent that Jim was improving dramatically. In fact, Beth, Deb, and the other sick teenagers seemed to feel better each mile of the way. I realized this was a characteristic reaction of mountain sickness victims as they reached lower altitudes. The disappointment in my heart lessened as I realized even more now the wisdom of this prayerful decision to take these kids down off the mountain. Jim would have had to wait another eight to nine hours before beginning the descent had I gone along with the party. That might have been too long a delay. Actually, as it turned out, Jim had pneumonia, not just pulmonary edema brought on by the altitude. He had been ill even before the trip and had somehow concealed this fact because he was so eager to make the climb.

Since it was Sunday morning, we elected to take a rest, and I taught a devotional Sunday school lesson. The side of Kilimanjaro indeed proved for all of us to be the "house of God," the Masai belief about the summit notwithstanding. Because of the great beauty and silence about us, God seemed especially near. It was truly a worshipful experience.

Before arriving at hut no. 2, we dashed for cover as a vigorous hailstorm struck. It lasted only briefly. About this time I noticed that Beth's face was showing considerable puffiness about the eyes and lips. I diagnosed it as angioneurotic edema—swelling about the blood vessels and nerves. In her case I concluded it was just too much exposure to the sun. So I decided to trade hats and sunglasses with my teen-age daughter. My hat had a much wider brim and my sunglasses were larger. She looked a bit strange in this gear, but I looked even stranger. The feminine sunglasses and a too small cap with flowers and the word "love" printed across its brim just didn't fit me. I might have passed for a flower child of a few years ago, since I hadn't shaved or bathed in five days and still wore clothing I had put on three days before. Happily there was nobody else on the mountain except my friends!

Waiting for the remainder of our group to join us at hut no. 2 proved rather monotonous. But things livened considerably when the climbers gradually filtered in, giving reports of who had actually reached the summit. My daughters and I rejoiced that Paul and Steve were among the four who had made it. Both had tolerated the climb well, with little or no signs of illness. Many of the other climbers who had turned back had all sorts of complaints. There were literally hundreds of blisters, along with upset stomachs, sore throats, stuffy noses, and earaches. They all lined up for Dr. Bethea and me to produce a remedy from the magic medical kit that school nurse Jenny Deal had packed. She had thought of everything. Had I packed it, the supplies would have been woefully inadequate. Thank God for the ladies in our lives.

We struggled down the mountainside, finding the downward trip almost as difficult as going up. By this time my calf and thigh muscles telegraphed fatigue. I also experienced some stomach cramping. But I noticed the kids weren't doing any better than I was.

We stopped at hut no. 1 and were given wreaths and bouquets— wreaths for the four conquerors and bouquets for the rest of us.

Straggling into the home of the missionary couple where we had camped before ascending the mountain, we had our first adequate meal for five days. It certainly beat the soup, oatmeal, tea, and hard candy diet that we had been on.

In order to get the kids back for school the next morning, we started out about dusk for our ten-hour drive back to Kijabe. Needless to say, I spent a great deal of time in quiet prayer for our safety as we traveled near Amboseli Game Reserve, where animals could dart in front of our Kombi. Also I didn't want a mechanical problem in that desolate area, and above all I wanted to stay awake, being so tired. I reflected on how this Kilimanjaro adventure had found me in a situation of utter dependency on God. I seemed to be learning the lesson that I had to lead a spiritually oriented life in order to be in constant touch with my heavenly Father. What a great way to live!

We arrived home safely about 3 A.M., my heart filled with thanksgiving for the privilege of spending five days with all of the kids on the trip but especially with my son and two daughters. We had spent a great deal of time in casual conversation and had a great deal of fellowship. Five days without bathing or shaving and going for days without changing clothes had not been terribly unpleasant to me. Sometimes I think I would make a good bum.

As usual, early in the morning our little ones came into our bedroom and snuggled up to "big hot dad." They didn't seem to mind the condition of their father at all. Kids have a tendency to accept adults just the way they are. Why is it that adults seem to have so much difficulty accepting kids just the way *they* are?

8

Safari to Orma Country

It had been eight long years since a physician had visited Van Davis's Orma clinic, since it was so far off the main roads between Nairobi and the Indian Ocean. The Orma, Van had told me, are pleasant, nomadic herdsmen who practice an enlightened cattle-breeding policy and graze their herds in the Tanya River District. En route we would stop at other clinics.

Now, in February, I was driving into Nairobi, the first leg of our trek, accompanied by Art Davis (Van's younger brother) and Art's father-in-law, David M. Huber, from America. In Nairobi we transferred our belongings to a sturdy four-wheel-drive Land Rover, along with five large cartons of intravenous fluids and other medications. We were joined, as planned, by two teen-age girls—Jennifer Frew and Karen Coon, both daughters of AIM missionary personnel.

As we headed out of Kenya's modern capital into bush country with me at the wheel, I fumed inwardly. It seemed so asinine to have two teen-age bystanders along on a medical safari that would be combined with hunting. Art's father-in-law, whom we called "Pop," had a hunting license, and that spelled adventure to me; two girls could be in the way. Then the heavy boxes of medical supplies were directly behind the driver's seat. Being an orthopedist, my thought was that a sudden stop or collision would send these boxes right into the back of my head. If our teen-age passengers had not been along, we could have put the boxes elsewhere. I resented this situation.

Leaving late from Nairobi did not improve my attitude. However, making our way toward Githumu, a drive of more than two hours, gave plenty of time for conversation. "Doctor Jorden," Karen said along the way, "I understand you're from Wheaton. I'm planning to attend Wheaton College."

"Why, that's just four blocks from our home," I responded.

Karen had a volley of questions regarding the town as well as the college. It became clear now why God would have us become acquainted on this safari. This girl would be away from home for the first time, eight thousand miles from her parents. She could face terrific culture shock and would need a friend, to say the least. My resentment toward our two pretty passengers suddenly disappeared.

At Mulango we checked in with Van Davis, Art's slender, wiry brother, about thirty years old. This was his headquarters village. He had several women missionaries working with him, including his wife. "We'll get a good night's sleep," he said, "and in the morning we'll hold clinic and again in the afternoon. Then we'll leave for the Orma clinic."

Early next morning I began examining patients. Two were patients on whom I had operated at Kijabe. One of these was a ten-year-old Orma boy whom I'll probably never forget. I had been to Mulango some months before with Dr. Allen, and there I met the boy. He had a post-polio foot that dropped as he walked. Evaluation had led to the conclusion that a tendon transfer on the top of his foot might improve his gait noticeably and certainly lessen the likelihood of progressive deformity as the boy grew. So Dr. Allen and I had driven the boy with us. It was the first time he had ever been in an automobile. I patted his hand on several occasions when he appeared to be apprehensive. We had stopped in Nairobi, I recalled, and I walked hand in hand with the little guy. I thought then that this daddy had walked holding many a child's hand. I glanced down and looked into a small black face with big frightened eyes that were trying so hard to be trusting.

Now my little friend held my hand again as warmly as he had on that trip to Kijabe. Happily, his foot was doing well, and he walked so much better than he had before surgery. In fact his gait was very nearly normal.

Following the afternoon clinic, which lasted till after 3 o'clock, we began our trek to minister to the Orma people. I followed Van's Land Rover, and after a rough and dusty four-hour drive, we pulled up at a campsite where we would hold the clinic. Darkness had fallen, and we put up our tents by the headlights of the Land Rovers. After helping Art put up the men's tent, which, typical of Africa, was done first, I elected to test my foam rubber mattress and sleeping bag. Honestly intending only to stretch out for a moment, I found that test lasted all night. A warm African sun awakened me early in the morning, and I apologetically explained to Art and Van that this was not a deliberate cop-out. I'm not sure that I convinced them.

Our teen-age girls had easily put up the tent for our nurse, Edith Lossou, and themselves. These MKs are very independent and certainly can take care of themselves, as I already knew.

After an early breakfast, all of us set about to do assigned chores. I helped dig a four-foot hole in the sandy creek bottom, which apparently hadn't had water flowing in it for weeks. This seemed like a ridiculous plan, because the entire area had been hit by drought—but much to my surprise water appeared as we reached a depth of four feet. Van explained that the water could not be used for drinking purposes but would come in handy for doing dishes and washing up.

Our hunters, including Karen, one of our teen-agers who had a license for zebras, were anxious to get meat for us. We set up a schedule. Hunting would be early in the morning, followed by medical clinic in late morning and again in late afternoon. Siesta-time would be in between, a must in this hot, dry land.

The medical clinics proved to be quickly popular. There were no unusual cases—just a steady stream of Orma patients coming for minor ailments. I marveled at our nurse, Edith, as she worked in the heat of the day with insects as well as people everywhere. She asked me to see only the patients who seemed to be beyond her care. These were few and far between.

During the medical clinic, Van Davis was busy with evangelism. He worked with small groups, reading from the Bible as his Muslim guide translated the words into the Orma dialect. The people themselves have largely been Islamized, though they hold to many tribal beliefs. It was obvious that these Orma people loved and respected Van Davis. His folks are veteran missionaries. Van and Art have lived most of their lives in Kenya. Van had worked among these tribespeople for six years and had demonstrated a great deal of love and understanding for them.

A chief from an Orma village sent word that a child there needed medical attention badly. All of us piled into a Land Rover and drove forty-five minutes to minister to the boy. I entered a small egg-shaped hut made of long slender poles bent into shape and covered with grass. I brought the patient outside for careful examination.

"See how stiff his neck is," I pointed out as I examined the boy. He was about four. As I lifted his head, his small body also came up, like a stiff board. "He has spinal meningitis and a bad case of pneumonia also. We'll have to give him massive doses of penicillin." Out in the bush we had no possible way to identify the exact bacteria involved, but penicillin would be the most effective antibiotic available.

The little boy breathed lightly in quick, short breaths. His muscles didn't even flinch when the penicillin was injected.

I judged he would have died within forty-eight hours had we not arrived with medical help. His parents agreed to let us take him back to the clinic in order to continue penicillin injections twice a day. He recovered enough within a few days for us to return him to his parents with instructions to administer oral medication for a period of time.

But the story was to have a tragic ending. The village people were so taken with the "miracle drug" that they insisted on buying the supply we had given the parents. The child died.

While at the village I had examined several other patients rather than ask them to make the long trip to our clinic. One young mother had two retarded children. Her love and devotion for them was very touching. An interesting sidelight involved a woman breast-feeding a child. She proved to be the child's grandmother. I had heard of African grandmothers breast-feeding their grandchildren, but this was a first for me to see. I did a bit of calculating. Possibly this woman had been married at fourteen or fifteen. She then could have been in her early thirties. At any rate she had breasts that were obviously producing milk for her grand-child. This was most interesting to me as a physician.

The Orma people fascinated me in a number of ways. They do not drink alcoholic beverages, smoke, nor steal, I was told. They have a strong family culture. Multiple wives are permissible, following the oriental pattern of wife number one planning the family structure—she helps her husband select his other wives. The number of wives is apparently determined by the ability of the husband to provide for his family. The wives and their children live in neighboring huts. Though this set-up did not strike me as being particularly dishonorable, I wondered how much confusion exists between the man and his multiple wives. After all, sometimes men find it difficult simply to live with one wife without conflict.

The hunting episodes proved to be interesting, though in some respects distasteful to me. Tracking various herds in a Land Rover was difficult due to the dry and dusty conditions. Our African guide was tracker and hunter. His Muslim faith insisted that any animal to be eaten had to have its throat slit before it died. Thus, after a shot he would dash quickly to the animal and slit its throat.

Technically, the animal was most likely dead before he slit the throat, but from a spiritual point of view this seemed to satisfy his convictions. The tasty, fresh meat increased my interest and enthusiasm for hunting. Without fresh meat, the safari food—powdered milk, powdered soup, crackers, bread, and a few canned goods—left a great deal to be desired.

Pop had a license for oryx, a large deerlike animal with beautiful skin and trophy-type horns. Oryx is also delicious meat. However, due to the severe drought, we had to search for a herd. Finally we sighted a herd of four within two hundred yards. Pop's shot only grazed one of the animals, and the oryx hightailed it off, leaving a small trail of blood. We were concerned, and Van suggested that we stop for a moment and pray for wisdom to find the wounded oryx. Following his prayer, our African guide chatted with him. Van broke into a big smile and told us that the Muslim guide had suggested, "Bwana, you ought to really pray before you start to hunt rather than after you have wounded an animal." This African-Muslim theology seemed hard to beat. We never did find the oryx.

Again, we spent a considerable amount of time finding a herd of zebras, with a mature black and white male. Van Davis brought the animal down for Karen, and this kill proved very unpleasant. The first shot paralyzed the animal's hind legs. He struggled desperately to escape. The second shot penetrated the chest. Still the animal struggled for survival for a minute or two. The wounded oryx and the struggling zebra again removed a great deal of my desire to be a hunter.

The zebra is a beautiful animal. The face mask is an intricate series of small stripes, giving the suggestion of a huge thumbprint. The stripes on the neck and chest are broad, with the largest, meeting over the chest, resembling a bow tie—provided that you stretch your imagination a bit. Stripes run over the entire body except the belly and may even appear on the zebra's long, rabbitlike ears and tail.

Karen asked me to skin out the mask over the head and face, apparently believing a surgeon could do the job with expertise. I entered into the procedure with enthusiasm, using my Swiss army knife. But the job proved to be very tedious. A plastic surgeon would be far more qualified than an orthopedic surgeon for this procedure, I told myself. However, with care I removed the mask without a flaw in about forty-five minutes, working hunched over the fallen animal. It must have taken me at least two minutes to get into an upright position; my forty-six-year-old legs did not tolerate the crouched position. For a moment I felt like an old man. Karen's smile and thank you quickly relieved much of the discomfort. I decided I was really a soft touch for teen-age girls.

Later, we sat eating the hamburger patties from this zebra, I had mixed feelings. Were we eating horse? In any case, it was tasty and enjoyable.

At another meal on this safari we ate Grant gazelle meat that had some little cysts that likely contained worms. Being the camp skinner and butcher, I simply cut the lesions free of the meat and turned it over to our cook. Another time we sampled dik-dik, a tiny member of the antelope family. At one meal we had soup that tasted as if the cook had used the petrol jerry can to carry water. We ate the soup with no apparent ill effects. There was no doubt, I was becoming a veteran missionary.

Our camping experience gave me other reasons to feel we weren't exactly vacationing at the Nairobi Hilton. The monkeys and baboons apparently resented our intrusion. Monkeys tended to congregate in the trees, chattering over our tent tops. They seemed deliberately to urinate on the tents. At night the baboons circled about the camp, barking loudly, causing considerable noise. Fortunately I was able to shut out their racket through sound sleep.

Evenings at the campsite proved extremely warm and sticky until about 9:30, when brisk, cool breezes would suddenly develop. "This has to do with the hot air over the plains rushing upward as the cool air from the mountains circulates into the plains," Art explained. Regardless of the etiology, I found the breezes most refreshing. The only exception was that if you were standing in the shower when the breezes arrived, that proved to be a chilling sensation.

On one occasion the shower experience itself made me painfully aware I was deep in the bush. The shower, incidentally, was one you got in and out of in a hurry; you hoisted a couple of buckets of water up and into a large jerry can with holes in the bottom and stepped under the sprinkle; when the water was gone, you were finished. Going to the shower once after dark, I jogged down the path, wrapped only in my towel. Suddenly I stepped on an acacia thorn, which passed through the sole of my slipper into my foot. The resultant tribal dance caused my towel to fall to the ground as I grabbed my foot. "Streaking" in Africa is no big deal, I decided. My fellow campers didn't even notice.

On the Orma safari we ran across the first missionary sent from the African Inland Church to this tribe. But he had fallen into moral sin and had brought disgrace to the church. During our clinic this man returned and spoke with Van Davis in a humble and repentant way. He reminded me of the prodigal son returning. We trusted that he was sincere and would once again become an effective Gospel messenger.

However, I had some doubts about his intelligence. He informed Van that his Land Rover had broken down eight miles from our camp. Van gladly jumped in his own Land Rover with him to drive out to his disabled vehicle. But they returned in a short time. The man had forgotten to take the ignition key to the disabled vehicle. Van simply shrugged his shoulders and said with a smile, "This is Africa." He headed back to the man's Land Rover. Van really loves these people.

Sunday proved to be a day of rest, except for a time we saw patients at the clinic. I spent the remainder of the day quietly resting. I had discovered that it is difficult in Africa to find time to get alone with God in personal devotions. On the safari the early morning hunting trips, along with the medical clinics and preparation of meals, had left little time for meditation. As I thought of it, I couldn't quite decide whether I was really along to drive for the hunters, see patients medically, or be involved in the evangelistic outreach. I certainly saw how it is possible on the mission field to lose sight of one's true purpose. The missionary must discipline himself to take time to read the Word of God, to pray, and to worship his Lord.

It took three hours on Monday to break camp and pack both Land Rovers. The long drive back to Kijabe was routine except for a near accident. Our Land Rover struck a longitudinal rut on a sharp S-curve, and it was all I could do to keep the vehicle from rolling over. God seems to ride shotgun with missionaries!

Arriving back in Kijabe after a long, hard day's drive, I had a sense of real accomplishment. But with it I had tremendous fatigue and a slight case of abdominal cramps. Maybe I shouldn't have finished that petrol soup after all, I told myself. But, again, the vigorous, enthusiastic greeting of my family made me forget myself. There is no tribe like the Jorden tribe.

9
Meanwhile,
Back at the Medical Center

Entering Kijabe Hospital one morning in April following an absence of several days, I suddenly found myself all but hugged by the nurse in charge, Rosemary Scott. "Am I ever glad to see you, Dr. Jorden! With Dr. Bethea on vacation, I've had my hands full this weekend, and that's putting it mildly!" Miss Scott went on to tell me that three patients had died and now she had another emergency: a young man with a badly smashed skull as a result of an auto accident.

I assured Miss Scott that I was certain she had handled matters well, that even if a doctor had been on duty nothing more could have been done for the patients. By now she had led me to the bedside of the accident victim, a young African man who had obviously sustained a severe injury. He did not respond to spoken words or to pain. Though there were no apparent fractures of the extremities nor significant injury to the chest or abdomen, cerebral spinal fluid tinged with blood trickling from his ear indicated a severe fracture of the skull. Intravenous fluids were administered (to prevent shock) along with oxygen by nasal catheter, but the patient died in a very short period of time. At least I could relieve Miss Scott of the burden of this hopeless case. No wonder missionary nurses tend to be mature spiritually beyond their years. The responsibilities placed upon them must drive them to their knees in prayer more frequently than most of us.

A young girl had been admitted with a badly broken elbow. The swollen arm would have to be placed in traction with ice for several days in order to prevent circulatory embarrassment to her hand. Miss Scott could have made this decision on her own, but again she seemed much relieved that a doctor was on the scene.

Like any other hospital, be it big city, rural, or mission, Kijabe Hospital is a place of action, drama, and often heartache. Occasionally there are the lighter moments. Several RVA students required casting for minor fractures or sprains. I began to realize that these missionary kids were unusually vigorous and highly activated, to the extent that casts sometimes didn't last very long. One young man returned with a totally destroyed walking cast. "I don't know why it fell apart; it just did," he said with a shrug. I had observed him playing basketball and pointed out the definite possibility that this might have contributed substantially to the problem. "You're probably right," he agreed.

A veteran missionary from Tanzania, Miss Lucilda Newton, arrived for evaluation. She had painless yellow jaundice, and medical advice in Tanzania suggested exploratory surgery. But Dr. Bethea and I felt that in her case general anesthesia with or without exploratory surgery might prove disastrous, since we thought her condition indicated infectious hepatitis. General anesthesia in such cases can be fatal. Laboratory work confirmed the diagnosis, and she was given orders to get plenty of rest for a period of up to twelve weeks. Liver disease tends to sap all of one's strength, but not Miss Newton's! She remained vigorous and active while in our hospital, despite our efforts to slow her down. Her co-workers had insisted that she stay at Kijabe; for once she returned to Tanzania, they emphasized, there would be no stopping her from working as vigorously as ever.

A visit with Miss Newton one morning brightened my day. She

had just received an envelope in the mail. Opening it, she discovered a 1,000-shilling check. Representing about $150, it was from a physician who had supported her work for many years. No letter was enclosed, just the check. He did not know of her current hospitalization. "God is so good. Through the years he has always met my needs in the most miraculous manners," she told me. The 1,000-shilling check would more than cover her hospitalization.

Now that I had been at the hospital for a number of months, the student nurses, all Africans, seemed to be warming up to my presence. Earlier they had been quite shy in conversation. Attempting to teach them either medicine or Bible truths, I noted that they looked down, speaking into their blouses. Now they talked freely with me and entered into the care of patients with enthusiasm. Their timid reaction to me was not entirely because I was American or a doctor but because of the fact that women are truly second-class citizens in the African culture. The husband tends to walk in front of his wife rather than beside her. If there are objects to be carried, the woman usually carries them. Sometimes she is loaded down noticeably, whereas the husband walks along carrying essentially nothing.

It was in January that tall, energetic Steve Ross, Paul's buddy from Wheaton, arrived to be with us, to work at Kijabe, and to help missionaries in the Northern Frontier District. Along with him came my surgical nurse, Rose Morton, a diligent woman in her mid-thirties. She would join Debbie in assisting with work at the hospital. Fortunately Rose brought certain osteotomes and rongeurs, instruments I would use for surgery on Emily, a pleasant twenty-three-year-old Kikuyu woman with marked knock-kneed deformity of both legs. She had developed this deformity through the years. The right knee was bent inward in what is called a genuvalgus of 45 degrees. The left knee was held in 30 degree valgus. Emily walked with a peculiar gait, crisscrossing her knees, by necessity, with every step. To straighten out the right knee would require a wedge osteotomy of the bone just above the knee joint. A three-quarter-inch wedge would be necessary in order to telescope the two bone fragments and permit correction of the marked angulation. In my mind I did the procedure at least a hundred times, considering solutions to complications that could not be easily handled here at Kijabe.

I reserved an entire morning for Emily's surgery. Dr. Bethea was to assist me, but he was unexpectedly called away from the hospital. I elected to go ahead, with the capable help of Rose and of Bruce Marshall. Bruce was a senior medical student from New Jersey who had come over to join us on a short-term basis at the center. Bruce's father was on the board of AIM at New York headquarters, but Bruce expected no favors. He was great to work with. Following a spinal anesthesia, I made a skin incision from well above the knee to four inches below the knee, permitting the kneecap to be displaced laterally. Then I carefully dissected all of the soft tissues away from the bone, since the large blood vessels to the lower leg pass directly behind the bone in the area where we were performing the osteotomy. Exposure of the area was surprisingly easy and bloodless.

A power saw would have been very useful but none was available. To make matters worse, our hand drill would not function. So I used the osteotomes and rongeurs, the cutting instruments Rose had brought, instruments that to a certain extent have been replaced by power saws and drills in the last few years. I completed the osteotomy with surprising ease, and the two bone ends fell together nicely, correcting the leg as anticipated.

It was not possible to completely telescope the fragments; thus internal fixation became necessary. Selecting two large Steinman pins, I planned to crisscross these over the osteotomy site. The only wire cutter available, however, would not handle such a large pin. So I improvised, using a rush rod and a different type of pin, neither of which had to be cut off.

Following the closures of the soft tissues and skin, we placed the leg in a special splint, since X rays were not available in the operating room. We carefully moved the patient to the X-ray room.

Technically the osteotomy and pin placement were perfect, X rays revealed.

After we had moved Emily to her bed, I commented enthusiastically on how well the procedure had gone under rather adverse circumstances. "Despite the long preparations I went through mentally, we encountered situations that I hadn't counted on, and we overcame them easily," I pointed out. "I fully anticipated that she would lose at least a quart of blood, but her loss was less than a cup."

A veteran worker smiled. "Dr. Jorden," she said, "we sensed your great concern for this procedure several days ago. We have been praying as a group daily for you. It was no accident that this procedure went so well."

I thanked her, realizing truly that this was God's work and when it is, things really do go differently.

Returning later to Emily's beside, I marveled at the beautiful straight leg. Emily, however, was coming out of the anesthetic and grimaced with pain. "How long will I be like this? When will the pain go away? How long will I have to lie here?" She brushed aside the cultural respect usually exhibited by African women toward men and lit into me furiously.

I reminded her that I had told her that there would be at least four weeks of bed rest following her surgery. She turned her face away sullenly.

Returning a few hours later to again check on Emily's condition, I was again met by a snarling young woman, her eyes snapping with hatred.

"But, Emily, look at your straight leg. It has never been this straight in all of your life!"

She looked at me defiantly. "But I do not like pain, Doctor!"

Eventually, fearing that she might completely undo the osteotomy site by her thrashing about with the leg in splint, I put on a long leg cast, molding it carefully about the thigh, calf, and ankle to give as much support as possible to the knee. Later I found a very different Emily. She had a bright smile and her warmth was apparent. Having taken a rather severe psychological beating from this young woman, I felt free to ask her why her sudden change in attitude.

She looked at me with eyes that no longer snapped with hatred and hostility. "Doctor Jorden, I cannot smile when I have pain." The cast had made the difference. Now she was the patient I had known preoperatively. What a relief!

However, because she had experienced so much pain, Emily would not agree to the same operation on the other knee. She left the hospital thankful for our giving her one straight leg, permitting her to walk much better than when she had come to the Kijabe hospital.

The case of Phillip, a sixteen-year-old Luo boy who earned his living by begging in Nairobi, caused me unusual concern. In fact, Phillip scared the daylights out of me. He came to us with an extremely deformed foot and ankle. Years before he had been bitten by a cobra just below the knee joint. Apparently the bite affected the peroneal nerve, causing paralysis of the muscles in the foot and ankle. Phillip spoke a tribal dialect that was unusual at our hospital. Only one person was available to speak with him.

All went well with Phillip, a trusting, smiling boy, until we wheeled him into the operating room and started to prepare him for a spinal tap in order to administer the spinal anesthetic. Since no one was available to speak to him, we motioned to him to lie on his side, curled up in a ball. Phillip could not seem to understand. I instructed Bruce Marshall to gently but firmly force him into the desired position. A moment later, now curled up on his side, Phillip looked over his shoulder, his eyes the size of saucers as he spied the four-inch-long spinal needle. He began to squirm, making Bruce apply more force to hold him in position. After Rose scrubbed his back, I placed the needle in the middle of his spine. Phillip struggled noticeably then went completely limp, permitting Bruce to put him into the ideal position. I thought that Phillip had finally understood what we were going to do. Fortunately, we accomplished a clean spinal tap with no bleeding or other difficulty.

After injecting the Novocain, I removed the needle and placed Phillip on his back. At this point, I noticed that Phillip was entirely unconscious. For a moment I feared that he was dead. However, examination showed that his heart was beating regularly, his lungs were clear, and his blood pressure normal. I had no explanation for his being unconscious. We proceded with the operation as planned.

Phillip remained unconscious for about an hour. Following surgery his legs were, of course, paralyzed for about two hours due to the spinal anesthetic. He would not speak to anyone, nor would he respond to my presence. The same blazing, snapping eyes that I had seen in Emily appeared in Phillip.

As Dr. Bethea and I discussed the case, we concluded that Phillip had fallen into a deep trance due to severe fright. His reaction to the paralyzed legs was one of bewilderment over what I had done to him. Fortunately, as his legs gained their full sensation in the next days, Phillip's brilliant smiling personality again revealed itself.

Phillip remained with us for twelve weeks. During a children's Bible study in Swahili (he could understand the language but could not speak it well), the boy began speaking in a strange tongue. We had not considered him a believer in Jesus Christ, but his outburst seemed related to his enthusiasm for things of God. However, that same evening, Phillip was overheard praying openly to Satan by the one individual who understood his tribal dialect. He also became difficult to manage, threatening and trying to attack other patients on the ward. When Phillip left us he could walk on the sole of his foot for the first time in several years, but we prayed that the teaching he had gotten would someday result in his walking with the Lord rather than with Satan.

The outcome of a case involving Giaconi, a small Samburu girl, brought a great deal of delight to the staff at Kijabe hospital. I credit Dr. Bethea for encouraging a decision that I otherwise probably would not have made. The little girl had suffered a badly broken leg when a boulder hurtling down a mountainside struck her. The bleeding bone protruded from the skin, and the girl's mother packed the bone with dirt and manure—not standard orthopedic procedure! Giaconi was taken to AIM's Gatab station, where the nurse cleaned her up and arranged by radio for a plane to bring her to Kijabe.

During my absence from the hospital, Dr. Bethea debrided and cleansed the wound surgically. After examining the X rays as well as the patient's leg, I felt the best course of treatment would be a below-knee amputation. This would eliminate the danger of overwhelming infection, which could be fatal. Delay in amputation also endangered the function of the knee joint, which is of utmost importance to an amputee. Dr. Bethea's thoughts were different. "The Samburu tribe does not accept cripples very well. In fact, they may drive her from the village. We must try everything possible to save the leg."

Thus we began multiple surgical procedures to save Giaconi's leg. First dead bone and devitalized soft tissues were removed. Over a period of several weeks multiple skin grafts were applied, and I saw a miracle take place. That little girl walked out of Kijabe hospital, to fly back to Gatab. How glad I am that I had a wise colleague who changed my mind about amputation! Paul and Betty Lou Teasdale at Gatab agreed not only to cover Giaconi's medical expenses but to keep her in their orphanage until she fully recovered. This is God's work, and things are different here.

The case of this little Samburu girl illustrates that surgery is indeed serious business. Few laymen understand the price a surgeon pays in doing surgery. The conscientous surgeon—and I believe the great majority are—realizes that he has a patient's life literally in his hands. He depends on the anesthesiologist and the nurses to use good technique. He depends on central supply to properly sterilize the instruments. Yet, in a real sense, he is responsible for all going well. So the emotional strain of the surgeon is significant. Surgery is never really routine. In fact, the College of Surgeons believes that there is no such thing as minor surgery. Even the simple injection of medicine can cause a serious reaction.

I remember operating on a ten-year-old Kikuyu boy who had never walked. His legs were bent, the knees at right angles. While I was doing a tendon transfer behind one knee, one structure was so displaced that it gave the appearance of being one of the hamstring tendons. I came within a whisker of cutting that structure. Somehow, as I examined it more carefully, I realized if I had cut the structure, I would have severed the sciatic nerve that was markedly displaced due to the severe deformity of the extremity. Cutting this nerve would have resulted in permanent paralysis from the knee distalward. Though I consider myself a careful surgeon, there was a sense of thanksgiving to God that this accident had not occurred.

During a second procedure involving the same boy, we noted that he had developed giant hives, suggesting an allergic reaction to some medication. This posed a serious problem. But the patient's general condition remained stable, and I completed the procedure. Again I thanked God, for the hospital was not equipped with all of the medication necessary to resuscitate a patient with severe allergic reaction. Fortunately the hives gradually subsided, with no untoward effect to the patient.

As I have already made evident, I from time to time found myself stepping out of my special field, orthopedics, sometimes way over into another specialty. Gynecology, for example. I had had some experience early in my practice before I went into orthopedics; I renewed acquaintance in Zaire with a couple whose son I had delivered back in Illinois. That son is now eighteen years old; I am starting to get old! In Africa I assisted Dr. Bethea in the delivery of several babies. But the most memorable experience involved Dr. Bethea, his only daughter-in-law, Linda, and his first grandchild.

Arriving at the hospital one morning, I ran into Dr. Bethea. "What's wrong, Ralph? You look as if you've really been through a wringer."

"Paul, I'm glad to see you," he said, mopping his brow. "I need you to assist me in a Caesarean section. I've been up all night with my daughter-in-law. The baby is quite large and in the breach position. Normal delivery is really out of the question."

Dr. Bethea, a board-certified gynecologist, was obviously qualified to do the operation. But it was a tough thing for him to do a C-section to deliver his first grandchild. This was a price he had to pay as a missionary physician.

I quickly got into my surgical suit and joined Dr. Bethea in the operating suite. Dr. Bethea's surgical technique was as flawless as his clinical judgment. The procedure went exceptionally well. It was a healthy boy.

After closing the incision and getting his daughter-in-law placed in the recovery area, Dr. Bethea and I sat down for a cup of tea. The strain of the night alone, thinking about the surgical procedure, showed on his face. I admired him for his courage and strength. But the ordeal was over, and he was rejoicing over his first grandchild.

Some time later I was invited to meet with the hospital management committee and three local African pastors. It was a real revelation to me, as one of the pastors, the Reverend Wellington Mulwa, presided over the meeting in the style of an American executive. Several years ago the hospital had become the Africa Inland Church Medical Center at Kijabe. The church was realizing its responsibility to supply personnel as well as finances for the center. Their aim was to bring the work totally into the hands of Africans. The missionaries were in complete agreement. Though there seemed to be no African doctors on the horizon, we all knew our African student nurses would someday be capable of providing adequate nursing care for the hospital. Practical problems, such as overcrowding of wards with men and women patients too close to one another, were discussed. Pastor Timothy expressed the overall atmosphere of the meeting when he stated, "We are not in the business of hospitalization but rather we are in the Lord's work." That attitude made me feel good, especially coming from an African Christian brother.

Meanwhile, Back at the Medical Center

African doctors, I concluded, would fit into the scene at Kijabe much better than someone like me with an American hospital background. I fought to adjust, but there were so many things in the course of a day that would bug me. I like to have organized schedules where at all possible, but here work was rarely by appointment, especially when missionaries would casually drop in for examinations. Many times an adequate diagnosis of a patient could not be made due to the lack of laboratory facilities. Should a patient die, we didn't have adequate means or time to do an autopsy. Records were often scanty, especially patients' histories, which are so necessary in giving proper treatment. Part of my assignment was to help train the African student nurses with regard to outpatient care. Not only was I often frustrated because of the language barrier with patients, but the item I so often needed was unavailable in the sparsely supplied examining rooms. If I were to work at Kijabe on a long-term basis, I decided, obviously something would have to change—either me or the efficiency. Likely me!

But I was to face an even more frustrating problem—illness. I found that even a tough character like me could be hit suddenly with disease and slowed down. I began to feel ill one morning as I assisted Dr. Bethea in surgery. I had played an early morning tennis match with Paul and came to the hospital bragging to Dr. Bethea that I had finally managed to beat my son two sets to one. At that point Dr. Bethea asked me to assist him, and I agreed enthusiastically.

In the midst of the first case I noted swimming sensations in my head, and a feeling of nausea was creeping on me. Since I was merely assisting, I let my mind run a bit. Was it low blood sugar? Flu? Soon I noticed perspiration popping out all over my body. Feeling as though my skin had developed multiple leaks, I had to excuse myself from surgery.

As I sat in the dressing room, my scrub suit soon became totally soaked, much as in lengthy and difficult surgery, such as the insertion of artificial hip joints. Veteran missionaries, with one glance, diagnosed my illness as malaria. This seemed unlikely to me, since I had faithfully taken antimalaria medication each week.

At home, with a chill coming on, I put on thermal underwear and pajamas and piled into bed under six blankets. The violent chill and a pounding headache made me feel absolutely miserable. The hair on my arms and legs stood out as if I were charged with static electricity. Even the soles of my feet were sweating. I wasn't sure if I'd live—or if I wanted to.

A few tablets of Camoquin made me feel somewhat better by the next day. Dr. Bethea suggested that I had a mild case of malaria. "If this is mild," I shot back, "I certainly don't want a severe case!" I remained in bed, reflecting on the values of life and other spiritual matters. It was interesting how spiritual I could become when my physical strength was taken away.

Typical of a doctor as a patient, I elected not to follow Dr. Bethea's orders and got out of bed to attend a concert by the RVA choir in Nairobi. Beth was very anxious I attend, with my tape recorder. My head felt a little dingy, but I was sure I could manage.

I taped the entire concert, but when it was over I looked forward to going home and getting more rest. However, en route home we came upon two badly smashed cars. All of the victims had been taken to Nairobi except one young man who had a few lacerations—nothing serious. We agreed to drive him to Kijabe Hospital. Dropping off our friends at their homes, I continued on to the hospital with the patient. A nurse prepared him for examination. When I came in to examine him, his eyes widened in disbelief. Was the man who had been driving the Kombi to be his physician? The African nurse took considerable time explaining to him that I was a doctor as well as a bus driver!

Despite the pounding headache and dizziness, which returned full force, I fell asleep that night. A few hours later, difficulty in breathing caused me to sit up on the side of the bed. I had never experienced breathing problems. But now not only did I have trouble breathing in but exhaling as well. Wild self-diagnoses passed through my mind. Malaria? Altitude sickness? Broncho-pneumonia? Pulmonary edema? Why hadn't I listened to my doctor!

As my medical mind whirled, I wondered if the equipment at the hospital was capable of treating my condition should it prove serious. Yet a peace came over me as I committed myself into the hands of Almighty God. Air hunger is a very unpleasant sensation. I was sure I would suffocate. Yet through it all I felt peaceful.

After about an hour and a quarter of sitting on the side of the bed, I suddenly had a chill. My teeth literally chattered. The chill passed; the difficulty with breathing suddenly subsided. I had free excursion of my thoracic cage. My headache was nearly gone. The recovery from this situation was even more dramatic than the onset! I considered divine healing. But I also understood that it is typical of malaria to have a sudden onset as well as a sudden remission. Nevertheless, I was delighted to feel so well again. Thank you, Father.

The hospital medical committee invited me to meet with them, though I was only a short-termer. It gave me the opportunity to get further insight into problems on the mission field. One veteran missionary woman had been called in for evaluation. She was known to have cancer in several areas of her body. The home office felt that she should return to the United States. Yet, as we talked with this woman I saw radiance in her enthusiasm for the work yet to be done. She reminded me of Joshua as he led Israel in the conquest of Canaan. He knew he was "old and striken in age," but there was so much land to be possessed. It was a privilege to see what a life of purpose and dedication can do to even a tragically ill person. This woman's countenance made her the most beautiful and healthy looking person in the room.

Janet and I were assigned to counsel a veteran missionary and his wife who were having problems with their marriage. This, too, proved an interesting learning experience. They were two great personalities, but they had had their share of clashes. Even so, they had been effective missionaries. I was finding more evidence that missionaries are people—with God in their lives, to be sure, but people with problems and feet of clay like the rest of us.

Coral, an eleven-year-old Asian girl, and her unusual case helped teach me one of my most valuable lessons during my months at Kijabe Hospital. Her parents had taken her as far away as Canada for treatment of a rare disease called dermatomyositis. I had read about the disease in medical school but had never seen a case. Severe cases are usually fatal. Examining brunette, dark-eyed Coral, I found that her muscles had almost turned to bone. Even the skin was very firm in some places. Her knees were bent in the sitting position. The slightest movement of her wrists, elbows, shoulders, hips, knees, or ankles caused little Coral to cry out in discomfort. She answered my questions in a crisp, military tone of beautiful English learned in a British school. Years of suffering made her a very courageous human being.

I carefully outlined a course of aspirin therapy along with traction to the lower extremities while in bed. This was to be followed by warm compresses and active and passive exercises. "Try this therapy for ten days, and then come back and let me see Coral," I advised the parents. As they were about to leave the office, I picked Coral up to move her over to where her father could lift her more easily. As I held that frail little girl, with muscles and skin turning to bone, my heart literally ached. "O God, help me help this little girl," I prayed silently.

Looking up dermatomyositis in a textbook, I realized more than ever that hers was a hopeless case. Did I dare ask God to cure a child with a hopeless, fatal disease? Somehow my faith would not permit me to pray this, but I did pray more for this little girl than I had ever prayed for any other patient in Africa or America.

Arriving for their next visit, Coral and her parents all had radiant smiles. She had improved noticeably. She had more motion in her arms as well as her legs. Her knees particularly had improved, and there was less swelling in her face; and she had less pain. I advised them to continue the aspirin and physiotherapy.

After a few minor chores, I made my way home, still thinking about Coral. My heart was filled with gratitude to God that she had experienced some relief. As I looked up into a brilliant blue African sky, God's voice seemed to speak to me. "Your job as a physician is to do what you can, to make your patient as comfortable as possible; but have you considered this family's relationship to me?" It hadn't entered my mind to deal with Coral and her parents about their spiritual needs.

"Father, give me an opportunity when I see them again!" my heart cried out.

I continued to pray for Coral. I was almost haunted by this case and somewhat bewildered at what God would have me to do for her and her parents. At her next visit the medical improvement was still apparent but not nearly as dramatic as before. Coral was bright, cheerful, and obviously friendly toward me. "She refers to you as 'my Dr. Jorden,'" her mother told me. As we talked, I recalled my encounter with Almighty God following Coral's previous visit, and strived to include God in our conversation. I encouraged them to put their trust in him. As we parted they showed a continued warmness toward me, and I had a sense of satisfaction that God had used me to deal with this little girl—in a small way physically, but possibly in a significant way spiritually. It was good that I had obeyed, since a miracle cure of her disease wasn't to be. A short time later a letter came from Coral's mother. Coral had suddenly died at home, and her mother was writing to thank me for my love and interest.

I suppose I will never forget little Coral. I came to love her very much. Her case served to make me commit myself more than ever to God in treating the whole person, to never forget that within the body is an eternal soul, a vacuum that only God can fill. In later cases I considered this, counseling one and then another when conditions would allow. Often, of course, there was little or no opportunity, especially in cases where there was a language barrier.

One day an attractive middle-aged woman of Austrian background came in for an evaluation of her right hand, at the suggestion of one of our missionaries. Joy Adamson, the famous artist and author, had been injured some years before in an automobile accident and now was seeking help to regain full use of her hand. I found her to be a delightfully interesting patient. I recommended joint replacements, a surgical procedure so delicate that it could not be done at our mission hospital. She had visited other doctors, but apparently no one had suggested this operation. Meantime I suggested that she try a series of exercises and I would check her hand again if she wished. She seemed grateful for my concern as well as orthopedic opinion. She graciously invited me to visit her at her home at Lake Naivasha, some fifteen miles north of Kijabe.

"Bring your family with you," Miss Adamson suggested. "Children enjoy visiting me to see all the animals."

"Thank you. But you should know that I have nine children."

"Doctor Jorden, you should be in jail seven times!"

Miss Adamson is concerned about overpopulation and apparently agrees with the idea held by some Orientals that after two children the father should go to jail. I have frequently commented that despite the fact I am a physician, only one of our nine children was planned. I feel that God has given us our children, and we have no regrets or complaints.

Mentioning Miss Adamson's visit that evening at dinner, I realized my teen-age daughters would have been thrilled to meet her. They mentioned having several of Miss Adamson's pictures as well as her books, *Born Free* among them. Sue was anxious to have Miss Adamson over for lunch or dinner. Anything. Just have her over. "Why are you so anxious?" I asked her.

"Daddy, she is a famous person."

"You've got me. Isn't that enough?"

"Oh, you are our dad. She is famous!"

A happening at the hospital had made for an interesting conversation at home. It wasn't every day that I could come home and get such excitement. Someday we would have to take a ride over to see Joy. The kids would really go out of their tree!

10
Good News for the Masai

Excitement gripped me as I prepared early one Monday morning in February to leave for my first preaching safari. It would be almost nonmedical. At last I was going to see Kenya's perhaps most colorful tribe, the Masai. I would join Jim Bisset, a veteran AIM missionary and builder of thirteen churches in Masai land, all active and shepherded by African pastors.

The family came out to see me off. Debbie had our Polaroid camera out to get a picture. Remembering that I had heard some of the children chide me for not being a very romantic man, I grabbed Janet, bent her over backward, and gave her a kiss that she'd long remember. (She couldn't forget it, especially since Debbie recorded it for posterity with our Polaroid!) The kids cheered for their "romantic" father.

Driving from Kijabe, I felt content that Paul had elected to stay at home instead of going with me on the Masai safari. I sensed that Paul had matured and was perfectly capable of protecting the home. I had been reluctant to leave a tired Janet alone with all of the children. Our oldest, Sandy, who had considered just a short stay in Kenya, was still with us, teaching third grade for the teacher who was delayed in arriving from the States.

As I bounced along in my Kombi en route to Narok, about forty miles west of Kijabe, I reflected on what I had heard and read about the Masai. Joseph Thompson, the first European to walk from Mombasa to Lake Victoria, encountered the Masai on his epic journey in 1883, finding them a pastoral, nomadic tribe, living only on milk mixed with blood, and grazing their flocks and herds at will over a vast territory. Early 1970 population estimates numbered the Masai at about 155,000. Largely in the fifteen-thousand-square-mile area of big-game country in southern Kenya, they struggle to find adequate grazing for their Brahman cattle, thought to number about three-quarters of a million. En route to Narok, I found myself slowing down to avoid colliding with some of these Brahman humpbacks with long, curving horns and pendulous dewlaps.

The Masai I had already seen while in Africa made me want a closer look at these colorful people. I knew of their reputation for their handsome appearance, especially the Masai warriors, called *moran*, stately young men who prove their bravery by spearing lion. *Moran* often wear huge headdresses, catching the eye of the young Masai women, who themselves wear huge beaded necklaces, and leggings and armlets of iron, copper, or brass wire.

In Narok, Jim and Charlotte Bisset welcomed me as an old friend. I had met them earlier at Kijabe when we planned the safari. Jim is an ordained minister, and Charlotte a registered nurse. They have been in Kenya since 1940 and were currently building the Narok Bible School. Jim, a rosy-cheeked Scot of about sixty-five, got his missionary call after he came to the States in his younger years. He gave me a tour of the school. His mischievous blue eyes fairly danced as he pointed out the various features of the facilities. "All the glory goes to God," he said, rolling the r in glory as a good Scot would. He had a big undertaking going, with several buildings at different stages of construction. Jim's dream of a Bible school where Christian Masai could study actually began in 1958, and here he had the dream coming true: a church, classrooms, dormitories, dining room with kitchen facilities, and teachers' quarters. Jim is a highly organized man, and I found that his buildings are really something to behold. The Narok area has large quarries which produce marblelike stone. Local workers hand-carved building blocks for the Bible school buildings, which will no doubt stand for many years.

"Our preaching safari will take us to Narosura, a small community directly south of Narok," Jim explained. "I have arranged for a truck to take heavier items to a campsite." The rest of us would ride down in Jim's Jeep pickup truck and my Kombi.

We arrived at the campsite at about 3 P.M., and everyone—there were seven of us in all—began helping set up camp. With no job descriptions among missionaries out in the bush, I set to work helping clear acacia thorn tree branches that were strewn over the campsite. Soon I discovered the sharpness of acacia thorns as one penetrated the tip of the long finger of my right hand. The thorn seemed to quiver like an arrow striking a tree trunk, and I surmised that it had struck the bone. As I attempted to remove the thorn, it broke off directly beneath the skin. I managed to dig it out with my Swiss army knife. But within hours the tip of that finger was so sore I couldn't believe it.

I smiled as Frank Frew, the AIM field director of Kenya volunteered for the honorable chore of digging the hole for our *choo* (toilet). A former bush missionary, Frank entered into the task not only with enthusiasm but with expertise. I helped him enclose our luxurious *choo*, putting tall stakes and a canvas around the stakes for some privacy. Then we put down a toilet seat and hung up a roll of toilet paper. We had just finished when one of the women went in and came out screaming. A snake had crawled right across the toilet seat, as if examining this intruding object. Frank killed the snake, but no one was able to identify the kind. Someone jokingly called it a deadly mamba.

Once the camp was set up, Jim asked me to walk with him to the village *dukas* (small shops), which were just a few hundred yards away. We passed the Narosura police post, as well as the church and school which Jim had built the year before. The *dukas* would provide some supplies throughout our week's stay, and Jim simply wanted to let the people know of his presence in the area.

One Asian *duka* owner who had helped Jim transport supplies for the school and church welcomed Jim warmly. During the conversation the man looked at Jim and said, "Man of God, pray for rain. We need it desperately." Jim chuckled to me almost in embarrassment. Aside he commented, "It rains almost every time I come here on a safari. They connect this with me and consider it a gift of God."

That evening we had a pleasant meal in a screened tent. Jim's safari camp was somewhat like the great white hunter camps, with many niceties. Frank Frew's wife, Margaret, and his seventeen-year-old daughter Jennifer, who had been on the Oma safari, made up the remainder of our safari crew, along with Jim and Charlotte and their son Bill, a college graduate awaiting entrance into medical school. We enjoyed an evening of lively conversation. For devotions, Jim read several selected Scripture passages. His heavy Scottish brogue, along with his obvious reverence for the Word of God, moved me. He closed with a prayer which seemed to usher us into the presence of God. In his prayer, he mentioned the need for rain, honoring the request of the *duka* owner.

As dusk settled in, clouds began to accumulate, reminding me of the story in the Bible (I Kings 18) of the prophet Elijah praying for rain, whereupon clouds formed and were followed by a deluge. Rain began to fall gently as we went to our individual tents. I had borrowed mine from a missionary friend and had wondered how waterproof it was. The heavy rain that soon came gave me my answer; it wasn't! The rain also was evidence the *duka* owner knew whereof he spoke—Jim Bisset, man of God.

The night was cold, and I snuggled down into my sleeping bag, zipping it up to my head. About 2 A.M. I suddenly awoke to the shrillest, most agonized screeching imaginable. The sound seemed to be coming from just a few yards away. I envisioned an animal grasped by a lion or leopard and gasping its last breath. However, the sound was repeated at intervals. Trying desperately to get up to look out, I jammed the zipper of my sleeping bag. In the confusion, my cot tilted, rolling me unceremoniously onto the ground. Additional shrieks from this phantom of the night unnerved me as I at last freed myself from the sleeping bag and struggled to the door of my tent. I overheard Jim tell Charlotte that it was a tree hyrax, but he was unable to see it. Fortunately it discontinued its love call. Had it been a dangerous animal requiring quick escape, I would have looked like a kangaroo, trapped as I was in the sleeping bag. Later I learned that the creature that had awakened us is no larger than a rabbit and looks much like a guinea pig. It is also known as a coney.

Following breakfast next morning, we were again ushered into the presence of almighty God as Jim Bisset read the Bible and prayed in his Scotch brogue. The day's activities were adequately committed to God, and we awaited the arrival of Pastor Paul. Pastor Paul is a Masai—seventy-two years old, Jim said. He had heard the Gospel of Christ in his early twenties and had been reborn spiritually, giving up a life of wandering and sin. He and Jim Bisset had worked together for many years, literally walking through Masai land from one end to the other time and again. "Pastor Paul has a great urge to tell his people of Christ," Jim told me. "He mourns their sin and longs for them to know 'the Way' that he has found."

Soon Pastor Paul arrived, walking into camp with a broad smile. His Western-style shirt and trousers were not color-coordinated with his coat in any way. Yet his sincere warmth suggested he was another man of God. What an impressive pair he and Jim made!

"The plan for our preaching safari," Jim said, "is to visit surrounding Masai *manyatas,* using our campsite as home base. We will go out in different directions each day." He went on to explain that we would visit the people living in these settlements, and Pastor Paul would preach a brief, pointed message of good news concerning God's love as manifested through Jesus Christ.

As we went out from day to day, each *manyata,* consisting of many huts, produced up to thirty women and children and a few males. Most of the men were off herding cattle. They listened intently to Pastor Paul and to the reading of the Bible by Jim Bisset. Bare feet and hands kept time to the singing of Charlotte and Margaret. Of course, I couldn't understand a word; I simply maintained an attitude of prayer.

In one service a young woman opened up a Bible in her lap. She had been educated in a missionary school. Now she lived out in the midst of nowhere as a Masai wife with two children. It was a moving sight, this young woman capable of reading and writing sitting with these simple, backward people.

I'll long remember the faces of the Masai who attended our preaching services. Flies crawled over many of them, but no one seemed to notice. Masai mothers breast-feeding their babies during services was a beautiful sight to me. One little infant only a few months old rode on his mother's back in the usual Masai manner. Being hungry, he literally crawled under her arm to reach her left breast. After finishing, he fussed vigorously enough to cause her to shift him to her opposite breast. How this little guy realized there were two mystified me. The Masai, I sensed, really love their children. We handed candy out to the little ones. If they dropped the candy, the mother would quickly pick it up, lick off the dirt, and give it back to the child.

Manyatas, I discovered, are often surrounded by acacia thorn branches as a fence to keep out animals. The long, low huts are plastered with mud and dung, one reason for so many flies.

I discovered the Masai social structure and life pattern. They have a close relationship with their children and parents. They honor their mothers and fathers. The sons will gradually take over their aging father's work without complaining. There is a sense of concern. Elders are respected. However, there is also a chain of command, or you might call it a pecking order, in the *manyata*. The very elderly, I was told, often are not given the protection of the acacia thorn fence. It seemed to be a form of euthanasia.

We visited the local government clinic at Narosura, which, I was told, had been rapidly deteriorating. The previous dresser (doctor) was a man who showed indifference to his patients. People didn't care to come to him. The practice of medicine is an art, not a science, I reflected. The doctor-patient relationship must be based on love, respect, and concern. The opposite of love in this case is not hate but indifference. A patient cannot and will not tolerate an indifferent doctor.

However, happily, the clinic was making a comeback. The current government dresser was a man of compassion, and he was treating about a hundred patients a day. He permitted me to observe his outpatient clinic. He brought in five patients at a time, who sat opposite his desk on a bench. Each patient stood when requested and recited his or her ailment to the doctor. When patients would finish, the doctor would turn to me and say, "anemia," "tapeworm," or "malaria." In effect, each patient was diagnosing his own ailment, for, without actually examining the patient, the doctor would jot a few words on a paper suggesting treatment. An assistant then took the patient to another room, where the treatment was given. Seeing a hundred patients a day using this technique would not be all that difficult, I concluded. Self-diagnosis may not be all that bad!

Gonorrhea is a major problem among the Masai. In fact, there is some concern that the disease could deal a death blow to these people. The *moran*, the young warriors who roam the countryside with the ocher-painted bodies scantily covered with just a loincloth or blanket draped over one shoulder, give much attention to their bodily appetites. They spend a great deal of time painting themselves and plaiting their hair into pigtails. They usually wander in pairs. When they come to a *manyata*, they can each pick any one of the women of their own age group and spend the night with her. All a *moran* has to do is put his spear in front of her hut, and the girl is his until the spear is removed. This way gonorrhea can reach epidemic levels in no time.

Like certain other tribes, the Masai still practice tribal initiation circumcision rites for both girls and boys. More than fifty years ago the church made female circumcision an issue, and in more recent years the Kenyan government has sought to stop it, but without success. Tribal traditions are hard for these people to give up. The operation is performed on girls when they are about the age of puberty. A girl will be taken to a hideaway and certain of the older women, under the most unsanitary conditions and without anesthesia, will snip off part of her clitoris. This heathen rite is intended to aid the girl later in having children, but the operation often causes serious complications at childbirth due to the scars that result.

Back to our preaching mission, I observed Pastor Paul in action as he held sort of a street meeting. Eight Masai women came out of a *duka*, and he asked them if he could tell them a story. They sat down and listened attentively. A boy whom I judged to be about twelve wandered by and stopped to listen. I was concerned that he would disrupt this Bible story of God's love. When the story was over, the women politely got up and walked away without response. The boy, however, walked over to Pastor Paul and engaged him in an intelligent conversation about sin and salvation. Jim Bisset interpreted for me and stated that he was a bright boy. I sensed that God was calling him to be part of his worldwide church.

As we drove to the various *manyatas*, we would be frequently stopped by waving Africans who recognized Jim Bisset. He had taught them, perhaps years before. He is not a man easily forgotten. On one occasion Jim noticed a young Masai shepherd boy standing beside the road and stopped abruptly to talk with him. The lad had conjuctivitis—inflammation of the conjunctiva, or just plain sore eyes. Jim carried simple and mild medications to meet the needs of the Masai as much as possible. Charlotte, being a nurse, assisted Jim in ministering to these people. The tenderness with which Jim dealt with this Masai lad with the sore eyes touched me. He looked at him not as a patient but as a person who needed to meet the Savior, the Great Physician himself. He talked with the boy in Masai. The boy responded, "You are my friend." He looked at Charlotte and asked Jim, "If I speak to her will she hear me?"

"Yes, she also understands Masai."

They talked for a while longer, about school and the things of God. Then Jim noticed an aged Masai man nearby and moved toward him to talk, whispering to me, "Wouldn't it be great to introduce him to Jesus?" There was no exploitation intended. Jim simply had a love for this old man. I think he thought that the lad had time, but the old man was nearing the end of life's journey. I sensed this was a good lesson for me to learn. There is a spiritual urgency about all cases but especially concerning those who are aged and sick.

On Sunday morning we attended the church service at Narosura, the small village made up of little more than the church, police station, government medical clinic, and several *dukas*. The church building had been erected a year ago by Jim Bisset but, like his other churches, was entirely African run. Though the service was scheduled for 10 A.M., the speaker didn't arrive till 10:45, and the service typically began promptly at 10:55. The church attendance averaged 158. A school next door had fifty-eight children enrolled. It was also a Jim Bisset work. The attendance of both the church and school was impressive, in light of the fact Masai resist change especially in the realms of education or religion.

The church service itself was very unlike church services I was used to. A large number of those present were children, sitting perhaps twelve to a bench. During the service children got up and walked about. Some, I realized, were going *choo*. But the motion didn't seem to bother the adults. The singing was brisk and enjoyable. The prayers were long and seemingly sincere. Jim Bisset, the builder and founder, sat back and listened to the lengthy sermon by Pastor Paul and the local pastor. The only thing Jim was asked to do was close in prayer. It was thrilling to see this pioneer work in the hands of African believers—Masai—turned to the Word of God.

After the service, I drove back to Kijabe. This was a rewarding week. Though I had done very little from a medical point of view, I had seen a nonmedically trained man touch the physical and spiritual needs of his patients with a tenderness and concern that was a good reminder to me. I hoped I would never forget to be concerned about the whole man in treating my patients. Coral had taught me that lesson.

Arriving home brought a burst of enthusiasm from all the family. Jenny, as usual, was very affectionate toward her long lost daddy. Krissy, who tends to be a cold tomato, also turned on the affection. (Her teacher told me that Krissy seems happier when I'm home, something I hadn't realized.) Janet seemed just a little bit unglued. She said she had had some difficulties with certain of the children. Paul, Jr., hadn't quite been able to take my place.

Within an hour of my return, the noise and confusion had already gotten to me, and I mentioned it to Janet. "But honey, you've only been home an hour. Would you like to go out on another safari?" Then I reflected a bit on how homesick I'd been for the whole lot of noisemakers. No other safari was planned for a while, and I was glad.

Just before we left to return to the States, we had one more contact with the Masai tribespeople. I drove Janet and some of the home ec kids from the academy down to deliver *posho* and milk. A drought had hit, and there was great need. Little Jenny accompanied us and did her part, handing out two packs of gum, which she divided into small pieces. I can still see all the little hands reaching out to Jenny. Happily, we also had some cookies, which we passed out along with the other food.

11
SOS from Lokori

The shortwave radio message was for me. Dr. Richard Anderson, a British-trained physician and surgeon with many years of experience on the mission field in Kenya, needed my services at his hospital at Lokori, in Turkana territory on the western side of Lake Rudolf in a desert area. He had a patient with a broken hip who required the attention of an orthopedist. Also he said, he would like me to accompany him on his monthly safari to outlying medical clinics.

Arising early on a May morning, I arrived at MAF headquarters at Wilson Airport in Nairobi well before the anticipated flight at 9 A.M. We finally got away at 11 o'clock, after loading supplies, including two units of blood for the anticipated surgical procedure. We packed the blood with the frozen meat, part of the supplies for the various missionary stations en route to Lokori, some three hundred miles north. More than usual, I was glad for Arnie Newman's pause for prayer; the instrument panel of the plane had been damaged by fire and certain instruments were being repaired. "But don't worry," said Arnie, a mischievous twinkle in his eye, "I've been flying this plane in this condition for a week and have had no trouble."

Our first stop was Loglogo, where we had a quick lunch of cucumber sandwiches. Then we set down at a familiar spot, Gatab, the NFD, station boasting a landing strip on top of a cliff. As we began our takeoff, Arnie brought the plane to a quick stop. A herd of cattle began to meander across in front of us. When we returned to the original takeoff point, the right wheel dropped into a small hole. The plane couldn't move. Unstrapping myself, I climbed out of the plane and, with the propeller blowing dust in my face, pushed the plane out of the hole and jumped back inside. Soon we were airborne and winging our way west over Lake Rudolf and Lokori.

Desert heat greeted us at Lokori. Mrs. Anderson, a tall, slender, proper British lady, invited us in for refreshments before I went with Dr. Anderson to the hospital. I knew that man is not to live by bread alone, but by this time my stomach felt glued to my backbone. So I devoured the snack of bread, jam, and lemonade.

I matched strides with Dr. Anderson as he and I walked to the hospital. A man of about forty-five with a noticeably receding hairline, and perhaps a couple of inches shorter than my six feet, he wore a short-sleeved shirt, khaki shorts, and sandals. Like his wife, he spoke with a beautiful British accent. He gave me a tour of his hospital, a building of cinder block construction, with about forty beds. There was no X-ray equipment; thus the diagnosis of the location of the fracture of the patient's hip would have to be clinical. The patient was an elderly Turkana woman. It seemed that the fracture was in and about the hip joint. Her general condition was poor, since she had been bedridden for several weeks. Due to the anticipated safari to outlying clinics the next day, I would perform surgery that evening. This would also, I hoped, permit more comfortable working conditions in the operating room. The evening wouldn't exactly usher in air conditioning, but at least we would avoid the intense desert heat.

That evening I scrubbed stripped to the waist and entered the operating room topless; it was still stifling hot inside the surgical cap, mask, and gown. Bugs and flies flitted and buzzed about the operating room. There was no apparent way to keep them out. Again I was impressed that, despite the circumstances, all was in God's hands; this was his work. His people simply hadn't supplied enough funds to make possible better facilities, but Dr. Anderson was thankful, I sensed, for what he had.

Surgical equipment seemed quite satisfactory, I observed. Dr. Anderson did the spinal tap and started one unit of blood as surgery began. I opened the hip joint and found the fracture to be well within the joint itself, so removal of the head and neck of the femur could be accomplished with ease. This would at least relieve the severe pain caused by this facture and would eventually leave the patient with a hip that would permit her to walk. In America an artificial hip could be utilized, but not under the circumstances here at Lokori.

The patient's response to surgery was gratifying. Not only was the relief from pain evident, but, more importantly, the two units of blood transported in the frozen meat container brought new life to her. But unfortunately no surgeon wins them all. Several days later the elderly woman was found dead in her bed. No one knew for sure what took her life, for autopsy was not possible.

After a late dinner the night of the surgery, we retired, anticipating arising at 5 A.M. for a heavy day of travel. It would be the beginning of a three-day safari.

Needless to say, I slept with no difficulty, exhausted from a long, active day. I shaved with water that felt ice cold, reminding me at that sleepy, early hour of the TV commercial "Thanks, I needed that!"

The next days proved memorable in numerous ways. We flew to such remote stations as Kalokol, Kapeddo, Loputulo, and Maron. At takeoff I was not sure which missions we would visit that day. Each station introduced me to bush missionaries who seemed to be called to a work of loneliness, isolation, and unbelievably long hours. The stress and strain on these people with regard to being self-sufficient and isolated had to be very great. I could readily understand why some bush missionaries have emotional problems.

Dr. Anderson epitomized the bush physician as a man who treats the whole person. His love for the people was obvious. He was taking care of people who happened to have disease. It is possible to be a physician who takes care of diseases that happen to be in people. There is a big difference!

Dr. Anderson and his colleagues all exhibited a spiritual emphasis in their medicine. Like other missionaries I had met in Africa, they consider it their primary aim to bring the Gospel of Jesus Christ to African tribespeople. Certainly, I observed, with the working conditions and the endless hours of work, there is no amount of money that could bring a physician to this kind of work. It most certainly was a calling of God.

The Turkana people, to whom Dr. Anderson ministers, number well over two hundred thousand and are primarily cattle people, following the rains to find the meager vegetation to graze their livestock. They themselves live mainly on berries, meat, milk, and blood. Turkana women, who have strong features, dress in superbly made bead and shell ornaments; married women wear a heavily decorated hide apron joined to a hide skirt in back, and the unmarried wear two V-shaped aprons, front and back.

The men are generally of a tall, slender, muscular build, and usually appear in loincloths, though they enjoy wearing skins and fancy ostrich-feather headdresses.

The Turkana do not circumcise, but they have an intricate and efficient system of age groups based on an initiation ceremony to manhood involving the killing of a bull by the initiate with his spear. Turkana, who live in huts made of sticks, hide, and grass, look upon certain of their animals as sort of deities that act as intermediaries between their souls and the souls of their ancestors. The Turkana sing songs of praise to them at the warrior dances and depend on them for marriage, wealth, feasting, and security.

Thus I could understand the desire of Dr. Anderson and the nurses who worked with him to bring the light of Christ to the dark world of the Turkana.

Their bush clinics brought an interesting array of patients. One man presented himself as a "herbologist." Realizing that I was a bone doctor, he demonstrated his right forearm as an extremity that had previously had five fractures. He described self-treatment by grasping a tree, pulling backward until the arm appeared straight clinically. Cowhide had at this point been wrapped around the arm to hold it in its correct position. From the appearance of his arm and from seeing him using it with no difficulties, it was hard for me to believe that it had, in fact, had five fractures. In fact, his clinical pattern now suggested to me that he simply had had a fracture of the carpal navicular, a small bone in the wrist, which would not cause a loss of function but would cause some pain. Without X rays, I had no way to deny or verify the Turkana "herbologist's" diagnosis.

Several patients came with opacities of the cornea. This north-western area of Kenya has frequent dust storms, and sand frequently becomes embedded in the eyes of these desert people. Local treatment often involves having someone take an acacia tree thorn and dig out the sand granules from the eye. This leaves scarring and infection. If the opacity is directly over the pupil, blindness can easily result.

Some patients presented themselves with symptoms of peptic ulcer or ulcerative colitis. There seemed to be a correlation between these patients and their jobs. The teachers and government administrators had a tendency toward these syndromes, which are so prevalent in American society.

Part of our safari required transporting two patients to another station. One patient was a slender girl of about four, who was obviously quite frightened. The nurses had scrubbed her, given her a fresh shampoo, and dressed her in a clean smock. After we loaded our Land Rover, this little girl was given to me to sit on my lap. As I lifted this frightened child, I realized all she had on was the freshly ironed smock. I only hoped that she wasn't too frightened.

As we bounced along, I supported the little girl with my hands.

She was so slender that I could feel her pulse through her chest wall. Her heart was pounding desperately. Putting both arms around this little girl, I gave her the squeeze of a daddy of seven daughters. Just like my kids, her anxiety obviously subsided, with a noticeable drop in the rate of her pulse. I guess little girls are much the same regardless of their culture or their color.

At Kalokol, we prepared to resume our safari by plane. Large drums of petrol were brought to the plane by pick-up truck and pumped into the tanks. It was filtered through a cloth. Flying a single-engine plane through a mountainous terrain with gasoline from this bush supply caused me just a bit of concern. Surely God flies copilot with these MAF airmen.

Loputulo was one of the newer clinics on our safari. The landing strip is out in the middle of nowhere. How the pilot found this landing strip was a mystery to me. Standing at the end of the runway as the plane approached was a large group of Pokot tribespeople. They stood clapping their hands and singing hymns in their Pokot tongue. As Dr. Anderson approached them ahead of me, I saw a picture that would be great for advertising missions. This British physician was obviously loved by these isolated Africans, telegraphed by their smiles and warm greeting. In the midst of this tribe were three Africans dressed in Western-type clothes. They were not only the teachers in the school system but were Christian evangelists. Dr. Anderson, I learned, worked closely with these three men. Here was pioneer mission work at its finest level.

After we set up the medical clinic under a large acacia thorn tree, the evangelists began a service a few yards away. They gave me the seat of honor, a stone about the size of a large cantelope placed at the very feet of the evangelists. It was a thrill to hear the Word of God presented in the strange tongue of the Pokot tribe. Glancing down directly in front of me, I saw six feet covered with strange shoes and stockings. The Bible verse came to me, "How beautiful are the feet of those who preach the Gospel" (paraphrased from Isa. 52:7). Only God could think that those feet were beautiful. Moving my camera slowly into position, I took a picture of the six feet that were meaningful to me and to God.

As we started the medical clinic, a young man came for examination, showing me a knee bent at 90 degrees. The joint was solidly fixed in this position. No solution was possible short of amputation above the knee. This young man had waited several months for the anticipated visit of the bone doctor from America. As I completed the examination, I shook my head sadly. I spoke to him through an interpreter. Obviously the above-the-knee amputation could not be considered by either of us under the circumstances. Nevertheless, the young man warmly thanked me for seeing him. It seemed strange to come so many miles to see a young man who had waited so long, offering him so little and yet finding his response so warm. This had to be God's work. We were not simply taking care of the body or mind but rather the inner man, the spirit or soul. I had a feeling that this young man was one of God's elect and would one day be called into his church.

One stop was at Kapeddo, a station covered by three Finnish nurses. Two were in their fifties and one in her late twenties. These three women cover the activities of a busy medical clinic, hospital, and school for children. They reminded me of the early verses of I Peter, chapter 3: ". . . pure in your lives. Your beauty should not be . . . outward . . . but a gentle and quiet spirit . . . precious to God" (AT). Though these women do not pay much attention to outward beauty, they certainly are beautiful women, quiet and meek in spirit and working to the glory of God.

Though the hour was late when we arrived at Kapeddo, we elected to go ahead with surgery. Finishing at 8:30 in the evening, I walked from the brightly lit hospital operating room out into the African night. Walking toward the mission house, I could see a large truck silhouetted against the night sky, with many men milling around it. As I got closer I saw they were army personnel in camouflage uniforms, carrying automatic carbines. For a moment fear gripped me, more than it had in any incident during my entire

African stay. Gathering courage, I walked on over to the truck, slightly behind Dr. Anderson, to inquire what was going on. The Finnish missionary nurses were standing eyeball to eyeball with the leader of this army platoon. Apparently there had been an attack between the Turkana and Pokot tribes. The army platoon had been assigned to investigate the matter. They needed a four-wheel drive vehicle to cross a flooded river in the vicinity. The only vehicle available was the hospital ambulance, and they wanted it. Though the army personnel were tough and armed, the nurses stood totally unafraid, discussing the matter with them. Finally, they reached a compromise. The ambulance driver would take the leader of the platoon to the river and show him a place where the platoon could cross in the army truck. This seemed to satisfy everyone concerned. I felt ashamed of my own fear in light of the obvious confidence that the nurses had in handling the touchy situation. Confidence in God in time of trouble leads to courage and confidence, and the Finnish nurses demonstrated this truth in a memorable way.

At Kapeddo, I was asked to see a tragic case, a young boy who had come to the hospital several months before to have the achilles tendon lengthened on one leg. During his stay at the hospital he had contracted measles followed by inflamation of the brain, known as post-measles encephalitis. The result was a terribly spastic boy who was mentally retarded. He could walk only with the assistance of others, and frequently he would throw himself violently to the floor. The repeated blows to his head had caused a large abscess to form on the back of the scalp. Using local anesthesia as several people held the boy, I managed to get adequate drainage of this abscess to lessen the pain and fever.

Crippled children have always been difficult for me from an emotional point of view. I thank God for nine healthy children. My heart literally aches when I am around a child such as that African boy. However, should God allow this type of problem in my family, I must have confidence that his grace and love will be sufficient.

Deep in my heart, however, I fear that I am not a big enough man for this "calling." Yet Scripture does teach that if God sends problems into one's life, he does send extra grace and gives strength to the Christian to cope.

I ended this medical safari in a most refreshing manner. Kapeddo has an interesting natural resource: hot mineral springs produce a beautiful waterfall a few hundred yards from the mission station. This water has been piped into a small swimming pool close to the station. After seeing my last patients, I finished the day with a dip in the hot mineral pool. This was even better than a sauna bath. That night I slept like a baby. But, come to think of it, I always managed to go out like a light on safaris.

12
Family Safari
to Pokot Country

The kids let out a whoop of joy when I announced that we were going on a family safari to the small bush village of Churo. Everyone would go except Sandy, our oldest, and the two youngest ones, Krissy and Jenny, who fussed and fumed a bit but seemed content to be with Sandy. (Our Debbie had already returned to the States to work and enter college.) This was a trip we had long talked about, one that would take us to the land of the Pokot of northwest Kenya. Since our arrival in Africa, the family had not been together on a medical safari. So this would give them an opportunity to see mission work in real bush country.

Since a great deal of camping equipment and food would be necessary for such a large group, Art Davis, the missionary responsible for ministering to the Pokot, decided that we would travel in two vehicles. Pilot Arnie Newman loaned us his Land Cruiser, in which Jimmy, Susie, Judy, Paul, Art, and I would ride. Janet, Beth, Peggy Clements and three nurses (Sally Allen, Rosemary Scott, and Mrs. Reneé Bigley) would follow the next day in our Kombi, driven by Bob Clements, a photographer.

Thus, in early May we started out on our 150-mile trip in the Land Cruiser, with me at the wheel, packed in with equipment and supplies. Art set the example for the kids by sitting in cramped quarters and holding several items on his lap without complaint. We stopped frequenlty to stretch our legs and eat snacks. Long ago I had found that keeping the blood sugar high helps kids—and adults—travel well.

Within two hours of Churo we stopped at a farm, where Art purchased *posho* and powdered milk for the people to whom we would minister. This merely added more to the already overloaded Land Cruiser. But the last ten miles served to shake down the equipment and supplies, as well as passengers, as we traveled over an unbelievably rocky and irregular road. We were really deep in the bush, and the kids kept sharp watch for animals and "savages."

Art had clued us in as to what to expect with respect to the Pokot, or Suk, as they are also called. The men wear ivory lip plugs and often a metal nose plate, but little more, except possibly skin capes and fancy headdresses. Their hair style is of the traditional red ocher and mud and often reaches down the back to the waist. A ball of ostrich feathers may be fixed to the base of the neck, and ostrich feathers feature as ornaments in the mud and dung pigtail. The women generally wear wraparounds about their waists, along with various ornaments about their necks. Married women wear leather braclets on their right wrists. A man may have as many wives as he can afford; the rich Pokot have four or more. Marriage is literally until death, with no means of divorce.

The Pokot number more than ninety-three thousand and are divided by area, one group being the people who have taken to agriculture, and the other, the cattle people of the plains. It was the people, known as the Pi Pa Pax, whom we were about to visit.

The sun was low when we arrived in Churo, a tiny village. Here Art had built a metal shed in ten-by-ten-foot sections. Imperishable supplies had been locked in the shed. The *choo* was really first class—like an outdoor toilet, except made of mud with a thatched roof. I got the distinct impression that Art believes his setup is like a Holiday Inn!

After setting up our tents and equipment, Art announced that we

135

needed meat. He had obtained permission from a local farmer to hunt on his land. Being familiar with this area, we would hunt on foot part of the time. Susan's and Jimmy's eyes especially grew wide, for this was buffalo and lion country.

While we drove to the hunting spot, Art carefully explained to the kids that they must walk gently and not talk lest they spook the animals. Our first stop and trial run was a comedy of errors. With both great rifles on safety and their magazines empty, Susan and Jimmy were given the privilege of carrying them. Then Art eyed my bright orange windjacket. "Dr. Jorden, you've got a problem there. I suggest that you either take it off or wear it under your shirt. It's too bright and may attract the eye of the animals." I elected to pull my shirt over the jacket. With Art leading the way, our hunting entourage made its way to a watering hole. When Art suddenly stopped, Paul almost knocked him down. Judy, Susie, Jimmy, and I all piled into each other, almost like dominoes. Fortunately, Art is a very relaxed fellow and found the situation as humorous as we did.

Since game did not seem to be abundant in the area, Art suggested that he and Paul continue on foot following the road to the south. Judy, Jimmy, Susie, and I would drive a mile or so and look for fowl or a dik-dik for food. Art carefully instructed me how to return with the Land Cruiser and at what time. He did not seem anxious to spend the night out in the bush without tent or sleeping bag. He seemed a little apprehensive as I drove off.

Driving farther down that road, I saw two yellow spurfowl just ahead. Using the open door as a support, I dropped one of the birds. The kids were really excited. "Shoot the other one, daddy!" My second shot, surprisingly, killed the second spurfowl. My kids thought I was Daniel Boone. They ran rapidly to the two birds but stopped quickly as they approached, their enthusiasm waning as they saw the birds' beauty. I gutted the birds on the spot and their enthusiasm completely vanished. "Just wait till you taste them. God meant that we should kill game for food." My comments drifted away into the wind.

Before returning to pick up Art and Paul, we happened upon two wild geese. "Now, they look like a real dinner," I said. But three shots later my kids no longer thought I was Daniel Boone. Unruffled, the geese flew away, honking their ridicule.

Art and Paul arrived weary and disheartened. "We didn't see a thing," Paul reported. The kids and I returned to camp triumphant with our two fowl. Following the menu suggested by Janet and adding the spurfowl, we quickly vanquished our hunger.

On this night I did not have to urge my kids to go to bed. The brilliant full moon gave the kids a magnificent view of the African night. Susie wore my long johns and Jimmy and Judy had on their ski jackets; the afternoon had been hot but now the night had turned quite cool.

Next morning Jimmy awakened ill, nauseated, vomiting, and feverish. After breakfast we had to hunt for more meat. So we made a bed for Jimmy on the front seat of the Land Cruiser, and he slept all morning as we hunted. We managed to kill an impala. We gave the skin to the owner of the farm, all that he requested for our privilege of hunting on his property. Art, I noticed, had a remarkable relationship not only with the Africans of Churo but with the surrounding Pokot farmers.

Returning to camp, we found a group of Pokot men gathered. Art had arranged for the annual meeting of the Churo school board. I watched the proceedings with intense interest. Art had made the board members small badges of felt, and there was an air of importance about them as they sat under a tree and chatted with Art and the African schoolteacher. I made tea for them, and the kids helped me serve them as they conducted their business. They had a rather nice school building, a low-slung adobelike structure with a thatched roof, with perhaps two hundred children enrolled; but the school board preferred to meet under a tree. With the board members dressed in various combinations of shirts, trousers, and blankets, it was unlike any school board meeting I had ever seen. Our kids could not believe that a small school out in the bush would even have a school board.

137

About sunset we began to express concern that the Kombi with the other members of our party had not made an appearance. We drove out to the main road, hoping to contact them. But finally we returned to camp well after dark, only to discover that Bob Clements had driven the Kombi in over the rough road that we had used. This decision was not without price, since two tires were flat. They were beyond repair, but fortunately we had two spares we could put on. But now the Kombi was 150 miles from Kijabe, with no spare tires.

Next day the nurses held clinic. Occasionally they referred patients to me, but most of the work required the tender, loving care of the missionary nurses, not the services of a physician. Between patients Jimmy and I spent some time playing soccer with the African schoolkids. Suddenly my stomach began to cramp, and I knew that I had the same bug that had hit Jimmy the day before. So, I was forced to excuse myself from the clinic.

After supper—two cups of tea for me—I retreated to the Land Cruiser. Janet and I slept on a four-inch foam rubber mattress in the back. Though the mattress was narrow, we enjoyed a reasonably good night's rest. That is, between my multiple trips to the *choo*. At 3 A.M. the door opened and Jimmy came in shivering. Moving between Janet and me, he snuggled down for the remainder of the night. He felt like an icicle. Typical of this age group, he had minor convulsions while sleeping.

At sunrise I awoke finding my feet firmly planted against the back door of the Land Cruiser. My head was down in the well between the back door and the floor, and my back was arched over the rear wheel cover. This was bad enough, but Jimmy's elbow was wedged in my left eye. Forceably removing his elbow caused him to awaken. Smiling as only Jimmy can smile, he said, "Sorry, dad!" I forced myself out to walk around, shave, and brush my teeth. As the morning wore on, I began to feel more like myself. Happily, it was just a twelve-hour bug.

Sunday morning we held a church service under a great African acacia tree. Our girls led the song service. The Africans sang enthusiastically, and we felt a real kinship to these black Christians.

Later, en route home, I thanked God for our great experience and the way the kids entered it. Judy, in particular, had really blossomed here in Africa. She had become a delightful young lady, whereas earlier she had been in a teen-age shell. Susie had demonstrated a real toughness in the bush, and Beth was talking about returning to Africa some day as a missionary. She was obviously impressed with bush medical clinics and particularly with such bush missionaries as Art Davis. I saw growth in the other kids as well. But the most remarkable one, I felt, was our mom. She had traveled these bush roads, camped out with us, helped with the medical clinics, and cooked. She hadn't shown any signs of illness, didn't seem tired, wasn't cranky. What a gem God gave me, I told myself.

Driving home with our family and the nurses, I prayed that we would have no breakdown, especially in light of the fact the Kombi had no spare tire. But Art had made the trip many times driving his small Toyota station wagon. Somehow I didn't have that kind of faith. Despite his faith, he needed a four-wheel Land Rover. Not that he ever complained.

After our arrival home, with the Churo experience fresh in our hearts and minds, we began to talk as a family about getting a Land Rover for Art. When we informed Art of our interest, he excitedly said there was, in fact, a Land Rover for sale in Nairobi for only twelve hundred dollars. Somehow we would get the money together. But our enthusiasm was dampened the next day when Art told us that the Land Rover had been sold. Unthwarted, we instructed Art to keep looking. Much to our pleasant surprise, in a few days Art reported a much better Land Rover available for a little less than two thousand dollars. We bought it for him. No longer would he suffer through the Churo trips in his little Toyota.

A day or so after our Churo safari, we had reason to be thankful for a roadworthy Kombi. It happened after a busy shopping day in Nairobi to replenish our supplies. Being in a rather adventurous

mood, I drove slowly out of Nairobi, electing to take the picturesque route through tea country. Though the road was tortuous,
the beautiful landscape was well worth the additional time. The
family was singing happily as we drove slowly around the curves.
Though there were no other cars on the road, I was driving at less
than half the usual speed. Suddenly a white Ford station wagon appeared in our lane. I planted my feet on the brake and clutch but
had visions of having my legs crushed by the oncoming car. My orthopedic experience seemed to suggest that I should get my legs out
of the way, but I had to stop the Kombi.

As the crash occurred, the front bumper of the other vehicle slid
over our bumper and penetrated directly at my feet. This caused
me to fly upward, striking the back of my head and neck on the
roof. Janet sprained her wrist supporting herself. Steve Ross's and
Paul's knees were driven through the light partition between the
first and second rows of seats. Though the kids were terrified, none
seemed hurt.

After managing to wedge open my door, I inquired about the five
people in the other car. They were also unhurt. Strange as it may
seem, this family was also from Illinois. You just never know who
you'll run into on Kenyan roads! The driver sheepishly admitted
that he was confused, this being his first time to drive in a country
where you drive in the left lane rather than the right. I told him I
could appreciate his confusion, that I, too, had trouble adjusting to
driving on the "wrong side." Fortunately he also had been driving
slowly and was bringing his car to a stop as the vehicles collided.

After exchanging names, license numbers, and insurance information, I discovered that our vehicle could be driven, whereas
the other car could not. So we piled the American family of five into our Kombi with our eleven and took our new friends to their
hotel in Nairobi.

As we drove quietly back to Kijabe, Beth quipped, "Dad, I am
really impressed by your concern for us in that accident. And you
were very nice to the driver of the other car. You didn't even beat
him up!"

Now, as our stay in Kenya drew to an end, we began to pack items we had purchased, along with clothing we would no longer need. Each parcel had to weigh less than ten kilos (twenty-two pounds) and be within a specified size. I also had to plan carefully how much more money we would need for the remaining days of our stay and for our trip home. I had greatly underestimated the effort and the cost of bringing my family to Africa and getting them back home.

About this time sickness hit a number of us, another indication that our family was becoming run down from their year's African safari. Some were hit with nausea, vomiting, and diarrhea. Then a number of us came down with upper respiratory infections.

Africa had been great. I only hoped we could hold out for almost three more months. A lot of work and adventure lay ahead if we could get our batteries recharged. I was certain God would see to that.

13
A Modern-Day Caleb

Having heard and read so much about Dr. Carl Becker and Nyankunde Medical Center in Zaire, I simply had to visit this great missionary doctor and see him at work before returning to the States. AIM officials obligingly made arrangements for me to fly to Nyankunde. Thus I arrived early one morning in May at Nairobi's Wilson Airport to await the arrival of a Missionary Aviation Fellowship plane, which would pick me up for the flight. But I waited and waited, becoming disgruntled but at the same time wondering if perhaps the aircraft had been in an accident. Personnel I talked with at the airport seemed unconcerned, however, shrugging it off as simply "some problem" that had canceled the flight.

I returned to Kijabe only to find Dr. Bethea in the midst of an extremely delicate medical-surgical situation. He welcomed me as a colleague with whom to consult; more than that, he simply needed a friend who could appreicate the predicament he faced. He was in the process of opening up a patient, a young woman, to identify the nature of a suspected tumor. Dr. Bethea could have managed the case alone but seemed greatly relieved to have my support of his surgical judgment. Deep inside, I felt less annoyed at the change in my travel plans for that day. I must learn to accept unpleasant circumstances more graciously, trusting God in all aspects of my life, I decided.

Later that evening I received a phone call from Nairobi reporting that the MAF plane from Zaire had arrived and would leave early the next morning. This required my being at the airport to clear customs by 7 A.M.

Much to my surprise, I was to be the only passenger. MAF had anticipated that one or two of my children would accompany me, but none of my youngsters could get away because of busy schedules. After supplies had been loaded, the pilot paused for prayer and soon we were in the air en route to Zaire. Not long after leaving Nairobi an unusual spectacle caught our eye: to the south Kilimanjaro stood proudly and magnificently, her snow-splashed peak clearly visible, and to the north, Mt. Kenya, at 17,058 feet another thrilling sight.

The flight took us over Uganda and on to Bunia, Zaire, where we quickly cleared customs. Shortly we set down at Nyankunde. Moments later a second plane landed, and out stepped Mrs. Venton, a veteran missionary who, I learned later, had come to the hospital to see if I could surgically correct her chronic foot problem. Dr. Becker had informed her that I would be coming to the hospital and possibly could give her the help needed.

I had read of Dr. Carl Becker in his biography, *Another Hand on Mine*, by William J. Petersen. So I had some mental impressions of this hard-working man of eighty-one, who had the vigor of a much younger man. A medium-built, kind-faced person, he reminded me, in attitude at least, of Caleb, Joshua's eighty-five-year-old friend, who felt that he was as good as he was at forty. Typical of Dr. Becker's attitude toward life, he had arranged for Mrs. Venton to fly in without having had breakfast, anticipating surgery that very day.

Fortunately, he set aside time for the surgical team to enjoy lunch before surgery. Lunch proved to be a delightful interlude; Dr. and Mrs. Becker were gracious and loving people. Their wrinkled faces beamed with enthusiasm for the work that God had called them to. I looked with anticipation to doing surgery in Dr. Becker's hospital.

Dr. Becker spoke of his long years of service in Africa, dating back to 1929. He went on to establish an inter-mission hospital at Oicha, south of Nyankunde, working there until the Congo rebellion in the early 1960s. He returned to the Congo (now Zaire) in the mid-sixties to spearhead the rebuilding of the hospital at Nyankunde and, in time, the establishment of the Inter-Mission Evangelical Medical Training Center, with four mission organizations cooperating in the project. In the process he was felled by three heart seizures in one day but shrugged them off to continue his work the next day. Dr. Becker told me that from Nyankunde AIM personnel service six outpost hospitals, including his old hospital at Oicha.

The hostess at Nyankunde compound, Dr. Ruth Dix, a charming physician, showed me to my room in her home. Her husband, Rich Dix, the mission builder, had built their home. It was designed much like a motel with multiple sleeping quarters, a large living room, and a dining room. Unlike many other missionary homes I had been in, this particular one was completely furnished, likely because it doubles as the compound guesthouse.

Ruth and Rich have an interesting marriage. Ruth is a very competent obstetrician and gynecologist, and Rich, a college graduate, enjoys the life of a builder. Their home carries out the biblical principle of the man being the head of the home. I found Rich to be a loving husband and father, and Ruth to be a submissive wife. Being in their home was indeed a treat.

Phil and Nancy Woods are two physicians whom I met at a Christian Medical Society Conference many years ago. Both are on the staff of the Nyankunde Hospital. Dr. Phil arranged a seminar for the hospital personnel and physicians, featuring orthopedic problems. Dr. Phil repeatedly referred to me as "Professor Jorden"—too heady a title, I felt, for a country doctor—but I enjoyed reviewing orthopedic cases with this fine staff of hospital personnel.

The surgical suite was small, with an adequate variety of instruments to complete a standard bunion repair on both of Mrs. Venton's feet. In addition, a badly angulated open fracture of months duration in an African patient was reduced and adequately repaired. The third case was drainage of an abscess within the hip joint caused by chronic tuberculosis. Surgery on the mission field does not lead to boredom!

The fifth physician at Nyankunde was Dr. George Westcott, a robust, happy man in his early seventies. As a young man he had served in Africa until his wife became ill. He returned to the States, and her health kept him in a stateside practice for many years, until she died. Since his children were not only grown but fully educated, Dr. Westcott returned to Zaire to "serve out the remaining years of my life in the Lord's work." This vigorous general surgeon travels to four outlying hospitals on a ten-week circuit. Each hospital is actively staffed by missionary nurses who save the difficult cases for Dr. Westcott. The enthusiasm of this man is contagious.

Morning prayers at Nyankunde Hospital begin at 6:30 A.M. After a quick cup of coffee I started from the guesthouse to walk to the meeting area. Deep in my heart I grumbled a bit at the early morning hour. But coming from a different road was Dr. Carl Becker, stepping briskly along. After all these years in Zaire this man began his day enthusiastically with his staff in prayer. In May, 1976, Dr. Becker retired and returned to the United States, mainly because of the ill health of his wife. Both *Time* magazine, and *The Reader's Digest* have referred to Dr. Becker as one of the world's "living saints."

My three days at Nyankunde ended all too quickly. Returning home, I flew with an MAF pilot on his mail route, stopping at various points long enough for me to meet some of the great missionaries in remote areas of Zaire. Leaving Aungba, we took two

Africans with us who were going to the hospital at Aba for treatment. It was interesting to observe these Africans in the airplane. I could detect no signs of fear. Their trust of the missionary pilot and his machine seemed very apparent. On the other hand, I surmised, untaught Africans do not often think in abstract terms. It probably never entered their heads that the plane could crash.

At one place we took time to drive through the beautiful forest country of Zaire. The streams looked familiar, resembling ones I had seen in African movies. Many pygmies reside in this area. I wished for an X-ray machine, feeling it would be interesting to x-ray their extremities. What doctors' don't think about!

Back in Nairobi I cleared customs quickly. The officials were quite friendly, seeming to realize that missionaries do not exploit the people of Africa but are there to do good.

John Barney, one of my missionary friends, was there to pick me up. "Should we perhaps go to the school rugby game in Nairobi before returning to Kijabe?" John asked. Rugby sounded good to me, so I "reluctantly" agreed.

This decision proved to be a good one, since during the game one of our RVA students sustained a painful and unstable fracture of his leg. Since no splints were available, I agreed to ride in the back of a Toyota station wagon with this boy's leg cradled in my lap. Then, after checking in at the hospital, I set the leg by putting it in a cast.

My return to Kijabe gave relief to Dr. Bethea at the hospital. Desiring some time in Nairobi for shopping, he left me to cover for him. In his absence a pregnant woman appeared on the scene with a ruptured uterus. Emergency surgery was required.

Perspiration popped out on my forehead as I prepared the woman for surgery. "I am a bone surgeon, not a gynecologist!" I told the Lord. "This woman could die in the next hour or so if surgery is delayed. This whole matter is in your hands. Guide my every action."

I began scrubbing my hands, when, much to my pleasant surprise, I looked up to see the smiling face of Dr. Bethea. He had returned to the hospital several hours earlier than expected. I gladly turned the case over to him.

At home I found our five-year-old Jenny involved in a most curious case. She had snatched a lizard from the cat's mouth, a heartwarming rescue. But in the process, the lizard had bitten her on a finger. Her main concern was the fear that this would require additional rabies shots. Though a lover of animals, Jenny apparently felt the lizard had committed the unpardonable sin by biting her. She took a paring knife and vigorously but without malice removed the extremities from the lizard, along with its head. Her older sisters were screaming at Jenny, but she continued her weird operation. I didn't become unduly distressed at her actions. I simply thought, "This kid would make a great orthopedic surgeon!"

14
Harambee!
—*Unity of Spirit*

It has often been said, "The family that prays together stays together." The Jordens also believe, "The family that plays together stays together." Praying together, playing together—an unbeatable combination. In Kenya we did a lot of both.

Each morning after breakfast, the only meal when we were usually together, we paused for a time of Bible reading and prayer. Despite the size of our family we almost always prayed around the table, even the little ones praying very simply. We prayed that we would live consistent Christian lives before each other and before others. We prayed for relatives back in the States and missionaries in the bush. We asked God to give healing to patients and to work through those of us ministering in the hospital. And there were prayers for such matters as Paul's leg, injured playing basketball, a tendon I ruptured accidentally, and Susan's hand, which swelled up following an insect bite. We prayed fervently for little Jenny when she was bitten by a rat and could not tolerate the rabies shots. If the smaller kids had known about it, I'm sure they would have prayed for a missionary's cat on which I made a house call to check on a broken leg that turned out to be an infected claw. The Jordens will pray about anything!

148

Probably our greatest concern for ourselves while in Kenya was safety on the roads. On each trip we followed the MAF pilots' custom of praying before turning on the ignition. We wanted our lives in God's hands as we faced the principal dangers of Kenyan travel: wild animals and wild drivers. We didn't want to collide with either. The collision with the Illinois family was enough, and happily not serious.

"Don't worry about anything, but in everything go to God, and pray to let Him know what you want, and give thanks." (Phil. 4:6, AT). This passage summarizes our way of life—in Kenya and at home.

Despite our confidence in prayer, I personally began to feel spiritually drained the longer I stayed in Kenya. Because I was busy with my work and other activities, and since it takes so long to round up supplies just to exist, I found perhaps less time in Kenya for private devotions than I find in Wheaton. My life verse from the Bible is Isaiah 40:31: "They that wait upon the Lord shall renew their strength; they shall mount up with wings as eagles; they shall run, and not be weary; and they shall walk, and not faint." I had to work hard to make time to wait upon the Lord, and at times I didn't work hard enough.

As a family, we found the involvement in worship services refreshing. Just to worship with other Christians, both whites and Africans, gave a spiritual lift. But the preaching was primarily for the young, uneducated Christians. So it was a great help to us to listen to taped worship services sent to us by Wheaton Bible Church, our home church. Often we would gather as a family to listen to the great choir of our church and a well-prepared, meaningful sermon by our pastor, Chris Lyons, whose New England accent lends charm and dignity to his preaching. It was all a real breath of fresh air to Janet and me and to our older children.

The time we took to play also helped keep our morale up and drew us closer as a family. Actually, play has always been important to our family. In Kenya I frequently found time to throw a football to Jimmy, Susie, and Krissy as they ran pass patterns. Or it was tennis and basketball with Paul Jr. and sometimes tennis doubles with Judy, Beth, Susie, and Janet.

We do as much as possible as a family. All of us will long remember our climb of Longonot mountain, an hour's drive from Kijabe. The kids climbed this rather unspectacular mountain as if they were tackling Kilimanjaro. Typical of Kenya in the rainy season, we started out in sunshine and halfway up the mountain a thunderstorm threatened. Janet and I got the little kids to our Kombi before the rain came. But the bigger kids continued to the top and got wet.

Sometimes the older kids have things to do, giving me time to spend with the younger ones. An afternoon hike I took with Jimmy, Krissy, and Jenny up to the railroad tracks proved a memorable event, especially for Krissy. We used a clothesline to climb a rather sharp cliff up to a ridge on our route. After it was all over, our thin, shy eight-year-old Krissy hugged my leg and squealed, "Daddy, this is the best day we have ever had in Africa!" To be sure, she had enjoyed seeing all the animals that we had run across during our months in Kenya, but she could see them any old time at Brookfield Zoo back home. Climbing a cliff with her daddy was something she'd never experienced.

In Africa some of our best times together were on long weekend trips or other minivacations to scenic areas. Janet booked accommodations for all of us on several long weekends in game parks. Like any family, small or large, we had our moments of tension. I well remember a trip into Amboseli Game Park that I took despite the fact I had been ill with what seemed to be a recurrence of malaria. After making all of the beds in our three *bondas* (huts), Janet prepared an appetizing supper over an open fire. To my disappointment, after I had driven for several hours obviously ill and with Janet's great effort to make us comfortable and appease our appetites, our bigger kids started arguing over who was going to do the dishes. My volcanic personality erupted, and everyone pitched in to help! Yes, we are as normal as the next family in many respects. Our halos often need polishing.

But, as a family, we had fun and adventure that only Kenya could provide. Driving out of Amboseli Park early one morning en route to Tsavo West Park at the base of Kilimanjaro, we came upon a single buffalo, considered by some the most dangerous of all the large animals. An angry buffalo may attack with a murderous charge that will shake the countryside. They've been known to put lions to flight in bush warfare. Keeping the engine running, I stopped the Kombi and viewed this magnificent beast through binoculars. He had curved horns and a head almost too small for his huge body. Passing the binoculars to other members of the family, I happened to notice that the buffalo was moving, seemingly stalking our Kombi. Expressing my concern, I heard one group of our kids urge, "Challenge him with the Kombi, dad, and see if he'll chase us!" The rest of the kids pleaded, "Go, dad, go!" I cast my vote with the group who wanted to scat.

As you might guess, with so many people there are countless details to care for in planning any trip—and our efficient Janet found herself in a bit of a predicament because of a forgotten suitcase. We were all ready to go to Samburu Game Park when Debbie and Jimmy complained of not feeling well and elected to stay home. Sandy volunteered to stay with them. So the luggage was rearranged. In the confusion Janet's suitcase was left behind. Poor Janet had to borrow underwear from our daughters and complained sweetly that she was wearing the same outfit every day.

It was on this same trip that we had a close call. Arising early the morning after our arrival, I jumped back as I saw a large scorpion only inches away from my bed. Capturing it in a glass, I showed it to the manager of the lodge. His eyes widened. "This is very dangerous."

How well I knew. Surely God was watching over us.

Our trip to Mara Serena Game Park brought a variety of family adventures. Driving directly west from Kijabe on the red clay road,

Surgeon on Safari

I almost gloated over the dryness. Rain would render the road almost impassable. The road passed close to the Bible school at Narok founded by Jim Bisset. I was anxious for my family to see this work, so we stopped for lunch with the Bissets. They received us warmly. I marvel that these missionaries could have twelve unexpected visitors—Steve Ross was also along—and keep their sanity.

After we forded a shallow river, we moved on toward Mara Serena Lodge. We found many animals in the park. We noticed a lioness lying about thirty yards from the road. Much to the distress of my less venturesome kids, I drove off the road to this beautiful beast. She was totally indifferent to our Kombi and our clicking cameras, looking off into the distance like a proud queen.

We drove for several hours before finally settling into the lodge. With six rooms available, Janet and I had the luxury of spending a night together apart from other family members. We decided we should do it more often.

En route back to Kijabe, we discovered that heavy rains had hit the Narok area. The shallow river we had crossed so easily on a low-slung bridge on our way to the lodge was now overflowing. It looked as though we might be stranded at this point. But when I saw a bus drive across on the submerged bridge without difficulty, I thought we could also make it. I prayed silently with deep concern. The kids wanted to try it; they were reluctant to spend the night in our crowded Kombi.

We carefully planned our attack on the river. Opening the back door permitted my three biggest girls, Sandy, Debbie, and Beth, to sit with their feet hanging over the rear of the Kombi. Steve Ross was tall enough to walk across knee-deep in the water, looking for boulders that might block our way. He removed one from our path. Judy climbed up to the rack on top. Our plan was to drive into the swirling waters, with Steve walking ahead to guide me over the narrow submerged bridge. We would go as far as the engine would take us. Should the Kombi stall, then all the older girls, from Sandy on down to Sue, would jump into the water and push. Paul still had

152

his right leg in a cast due to a basketball injury and could not help. However, he would be set to steer if the girls needed my help.

We paused for a moment of fervent prayer. Then, putting the Kombi in low gear, I eased it into the river and kept the throttle racing by slipping the clutch. The water was well above the exhaust, making our Kombi sound like a high-speed motor boat. All went well until the front wheels were out of the water on the opposite bank. At this point the engine stalled. My kids hit the water instantly and quickly pushed the Kombi onto dry land.

A pick-up truck going the opposite direction stalled in the middle of the stream. Though several African men sat in the back of the pick-up, my five daughters and Steve rushed to the rescue and pushed it across. *"Harambee! Harambee!"* ("unity of spirit"— Kenya's motto) they shouted, their fists in the air as they finished the task. The African men watched my daughters, amused and amazed. They didn't understand how strong my kids are when they work together. After helping two more vehicles across and finishing each job with, *"Harambee! Harambee!"* my daughters and Steve returned to our Kombi. They felt good about being able to help. I was proud of my kids.

Crossing the river was one problem. The second was the condition of the road to Kijabe. Whereas it had been dusty dry earlier, now it was red gumbo! In addition to the problem of keeping the Kombi moving, I had great difficulty simply keeping it on the road. Sensing the tenseness of the situation, my kids burst into a triumphant song. Plowing on through the sea of mud and into the darkness of the night, we sang every hymn and chorus that we could remember. "Faith is the victory . . . that overcomes the world," and scores of others.

We arrived home, happy in heart, thankful for God's mercies.

Christmas in Kenya presented a challenge to us as a family in many ways. Here we were in a strange land, far from relatives and friends back home. The weather was pleasant and warm, so different from the white Christmases we had known back in Wheaton.

I could sense a homesickness and loneliness tugging at the hearts of some of the kids, and even Janet and I had nostalgic feelings about it all. At one point on Christmas Eve apparently all of this was subconsciously building up tension, and some of the kids got into a heated scrap—about what, I don't remember.

As I considered these things, it seemed obvious that, as head of my home, I should do something. "Hey, everybody, let's get together and talk. Christmas is supposed to be a time of peace and goodwill."

As the kids gathered in the dining room around the table with Janet at my side, I turned to the Christmas story in Luke and read that familiar portion. Then we began to talk about priorities and keeping our values straight. "God's highest priority was to bring us to himself through his Son. . . . He loved us so much he sent Jesus. If we are really members of God's family through our trust in Jesus, then certainly we should be living like God's people, and showing love one toward another." I don't remember my exact words, but I tried to summarize the meaning of Christmas in relation to our family at that point in time. A sense of peace and tranquility seemed to settle over us, though we still felt far away from loved ones and the white Christmas of Illinois. We paused for a round of prayer including very short prayers from the little ones: "God, bless grandpa and grandma." "Bless our friends at home." "Help us to have a good Christmas here in Africa."

Typical of the practice of medicine, about this time I was called to the hospital to treat a woman for severe hand injuries. She had been walking a cow or bull through a pasture, a rope tied to the animal wrapped about her hand. She fell and the animal ran, dragging her behind. As the rope slipped from her fingers, it tore off two fingers and mangled others. I did surgery on her as my family waited at home.

As much as possible we had tried to create a Christmas atmosphere at home. Two missionary boys had graciously dropped off a freshly cut cypress evergreen they had brought from the forest. Having no stand, I hit on the idea of suspending the tree with a rope from an overhead beam, the base dangling into a bucket of water. The kids helped decorate it with Christmas cards and strings of popcorn. Except for the lack of lights and colorful tree ornaments, our tree didn't look bad at all. Unlike any tree we had ever had, it turned with the slightest motion as it dangled from the beam.

Awakening early Christmas morning, we tried to forget the summerlike weather as we gathered about the ever-turning tree to open presents. Our gifts were not as many as usual, and they were simpler. Our remarkable mom had bought the gifts, mainly in Nairobi, with little help from me. Some of our gifts were wrapped in Christmas paper given to us by missionary friends, some of whom have the frugal habit of carefully removing wrappings from gifts and ironing it for the next year. However, we tore into gifts in typical American style. There was a new dress for Sandy made from material with a colorful, flowery print and simply styled after the kimonolike dresses worn by many African women. Debbie and Beth, our seamstresses, received material for new dresses. And the younger children treasured books and clothing. Judy and I received identical pictures of African scenes, with mine attractively framed. As the morning wore on, Judy inadvertently sat on my pictures, breaking the glass of one. This was too much for Janet, she had to leave the room for a time, becoming a bit unglued over Judy's carelessness.

But all was forgiven by dinnertime as Janet served up an old-fashioned meal completely from scratch. Twice in Kenya we had turkey, a real luxury in that land. We had our first one for Thanksgiving, then at Christmas we tore into a big twenty-pounder. We had almost everything else you might expect, including Janet's savory dressing and freshly baked bread—but no cranberry sauce. There were twenty of us in all: our eleven, the Tony Dickenses and their four children, and Mrs. Jon Allen and her two children (Dr. Allen was working in the Northern Frontier, unable to get back for Christmas due to transportation problems).

Surgeon on Safari

Our Christmas was made even happier with visits from other missionaries who stopped to give us gifts, usually homemade cookies, cake, or candy. They brought Christmas cards, some admittedly saved from the previous year, with original signatures erased. It moved us to see these people on such limited incomes take the time and effort to express their love. And I mustn't forget the groups of Africans coming to the door to sing carols, some in English, others in Kikuyu. We were fascinated to hear and watch them. They sang so enthusiastically, their beautiful black skin accenting white teeth and brilliant eyes. We offered them cookies, which they devoured. I got the feeling we were being serenaded by the same people at times because they enjoyed the rewards. But their coming reminded me that the greatest story ever told is not just for Americans but for Africans as well; yes, for peoples of every color and tongue around the world.

Our vacation trip to Mombasa, Kenya's principal seaport town on the Indian Ocean, proved an exciting experience for all of us and saw the Jordens in a variety of moods.

I got off to a bad start on this trip. Before dawn we all carried our luggage out to the Kombi, anticipating a three-hundred-mile trip and wanting an early start. I tossed some of the heavier pieces on top and climbed up in order to tie them to the overhead carrier. I called for someone to begin handing up other items, but all was quiet. Everyone had disappeared. Bursting into the dining room, I found my entire family sitting at the breakfast table. "Hi, dad, where've you been? Breakfast is getting cold." The farthest thing from their minds was their father perched on top of the Kombi.

Approaching Mombasa that afternoon, I pulled the Kombi over, seeing heavy clouds ahead. "Hey, gang, let's get the luggage down and inside the Kombi," I ordered. As we worked, there was some muttering about the cramped quarters and "besides, it isn't going to rain." We resumed our travel only to run into a sudden downpour of rain within a mile. The muttering ceased.

I had been glancing somewhat scornfully at Paul, who had slept most of the way to Mombasa. Having been up late the preceding two nights, he was catching up on sleep. He hadn't been any help up to now; I only hoped he would be awake and moving when it came time to unpack the car.

Happily, he did manage to exert himself just enough to keep my temper down as we unloaded our belongings into a missionary guesthouse on the beach at a place called Mizpah. These inexpensive accommodations left much to be desired. For one thing, the mattresses appeared to be relics from the Dark Ages. But we could have been paying exorbitat prices somewhere else; this thought and the beach and ocean, breathtaking in their beauty, made us quite satisfied. The crystal-clear blue water, studded with coral, and the white sand proved to be a playground of immense beauty and pleasure.

Wearing gym shoes, as instructed by veteran missionaries, we took our first swim. It was like a warm salt bath with great breakers massaging our bodies. The only unpleasant things were the jutting pieces of coral that made the gym shoes necessary.

That evening, as we prepared for early bedtime, I carefully tucked our little ones into their ancient beds with rather inadequate mosquito netting. Suddenly I noticed Paul, sound asleep on a cot. He was still wearing his swimming trunks and tennis shoes. With malaria a threat, I had been spraying mosquito repellent on the children. Turning to Paul, I began to spray his arms, legs, and back. Suddenly he was on his feet, smiling in his good-natured way. "OK, OK, dad, I'll do it. I'll do it! What do you want me to do?" In the stupor of deep sleep, my son must have been recalling the afternoon trip where his slowness in responding to my requests led to frustration. We all had a good laugh, Paul included.

The following day our missionary friends the Tony Dickenses arrived from Kijabe. They set up tents for their group in front of the cottage next door. We enjoyed them and were shocked one morning when they reported that all their money—five hundred shillings, or seventy-five dollars—and other valuables had been taken during the night from the tent where they slept.

Later, we held a family conference. Originally, we had expected to pay up to $140 a day here at Mombasa, but then we had obtained the inexpensive accommodations. "It seems to me that the Lord would have us help the Dickenses in their loss," I suggested. "Maybe we can even replace the 500 shillings, if everyone is willing to make sacrifices." The kids were in complete agreement.

On informing Tony of our family's decision, he warmly squeezed my shoulder and, looking me squarely in the eye, said quietly, "Thank you."

After a vigorous afternoon swim, our family dressed for supper. "Hey, dad, how about taking us out for dinner?" someone urged. Their personal sacrifice on behalf of the Dickenses did not last very long! Not only did we eat out that evening as a family, but we took the Dickenses out also. God had more than met our needs. We just felt it was great to be part of the AIM missionary family.

While at Mombasa, I had an adventure with Jimmy. Our cabin was furnished with some inner tubes as well as goggles, snorkels, and a spear gun. So Jimmy and I went spear fishing, with me swimming and Jimmy floating on the inner tube. Sighting an octopus along the reef, Jimmy and I decided to try to spear it. Much to my surprise, I hit it. But then it began thrashing about toward me. I hastily swam for shore, shouting to Jimmy to get out of the area. My Scottish heart would not let me drop the spear gun. I thought I had a monster till I got it ashore. It was only three feet in diameter. I had pierced its shoulder in a nonvital spot and managed to shake it loose from the spear. The octopus quickly made its way back to the reef, seemingly no worse for the wound.

An incident at Jadini Beach Hotel where we went for a buffet lunch and a swim brought laughs but also showed that I am not as big and strong as I sometimes think I am. Our girls were changing in the woman's washroom. I went with Paul and Jimmy into the men's washroom immediately adjacent to where the girls were dressing. Noticing a door that I thought led into the women's washroom, I made sure it was bolted, not wanting the girls to wander into the men's room and be embarrassed. Having changed to my suit,

I carried my clothes to the Kombi only to hear my daughter Judy call for assistance. She was having trouble zippering her suit. Having finished helping her, I heard a loud pounding inside. It dawned on me that I may have made an error.

I quickly unbolted the door to come face to face with a large and irate African. "Someone locked the door on me while I was in the toilet," he exclaimed, so angry he was literally shaking.

"How could anyone be so stupid as to lock a man in a stall from the outside?" I responded. I also suggested that it was very fortunate for him that I had happened to come along!

Smiling now, the big African shook my hand warmly and went his way. All that I told him was very true. I didn't tell him more because I was concerned that my nine children have a living father.

Later, as we said good-bye to Mombasa and headed back to Kijabe, our kids began to quietly sing. We lack harmony as a family but not enthusiasm. Our hearts were filled with gratitude to God for such a marvelous vacation in this strange and beautiful country. Comments along this line led our family to speak of the beauty of our own land and to sing "America." I began to get a lump in my throat, as at Fourth of July parades. Maybe I was getting a bit homesick, too.

15
Safari's End

To the delight of our kids, Rift Valley Academy is rather ecumenical in observance of holidays; not only are Kenyan holidays observed, but school closes for many Canadian and American special days, July the Fourth included. They refer to it as *Uhuru Day*, meaning "freedom" day. So, with the kids free, on July 4 most of our family piled into our Kombi to drive to Lake Naivasha to make a call on Joy Adamson. I had put Joy on an exercise program to see if she could regain better use of her injured hand. But admittedly it was more than a routine medical call; the children, especially the teen-age girls. Sue—a real animal lover—Judy, and Beth, had been dying to meet her.

Arriving at her home, we called to an African worker, informing him that we wished to see Miss Adamson. We waited on the porch of her ranch-style house. On the wall were pictures of animals, including Elsa, the lion of *Born Free* fame. The setting was indeed lovely. All was quiet and serene, the silence broken only by the songs of birds. The house was completely isolated. The waters of Lake Naivasha sparkled through the foliage. What a perfect spot for Joy Adamson to write and spend uninterrupted hours painting, to add to her countless works on Kenyan life.

Soon an attractive woman greeted us in a British accent. She introduced herself as Miss Adamson's secretary. I explained the reason for our visit, and she disappeared into the house. Our visit was completely unexpected, since Miss Adamson's phone was out of order. But presently my charming patient came out to the porch, smiling. She greeted us warmly. She explained that she was somewhat incapacitated, having fallen two weeks prior to our visit, fracturing her right elbow and injuring toes of her left foot. Her husband, George, was out as usual, on a safari somewhere in connection with his work.

I examined her hand and asked her to demonstrate how well she could use it. I detected slight improvement through the exercises, but encouraged her to follow through with the operation I had suggested—joint replacements. She said she would likely have the work done in England.

As we visited further, Miss Adamson's secretary served us tea and cookies. Joy showed us several interesting rooms in her home and we admired her striking paintings and photographs on the walls. On display also was a poster advertising *Born Free*.

While the kids entertained themselves, Joy chatted with Janet and me, telling us about her involvement in producing the "Born Free" series. She was especially interested in our views of what Americans would enjoy in connection with the film presentations. As she talked, I was convinced that Joy Adamson has a deep love for Kenya, its peoples and animal life. The TV series wasn't just a commercial thing in her mind but, more importantly, a way to emphasize conservation and to share with the world her wonderful Kenya.

Though we had planned only a short visit, we sat enthralled as she talked of Africa's traditions and especially of her intense interest in animals. Though she often had had animals at her home, she had none at this particular time. Joy, we discovered, is a religious person, considering God's great outdoors her cathedral. We talked of the need to know God personally through his Son, and these spiritual thoughts seemed to be well received.

Miss Adamson's interest in Kenya extended to the medical field. "I would urge you, Dr. Jorden," she said, "to consider staying in Kenya for a longer period of time. We need orthopedic surgeons badly."

"That would not be difficult for me to do should I feel that God really wants me here," I assured her.

"But, Dr. Jorden," she said with a twinkling eye surveying my large family, "I still think you ought to be in jail for having so many children. It's simply criminal!"

I smiled, holding my head high. "I appreciate your viewpoint, but I consider every one of these children a gift from God." We had been over all that when I first met her. She just had to get another lick in.

As we left, Miss Adamson presented the children with porcupine quills, postcards bearing her artwork, and other mementos of our visit with her.

Back at the hospital, I began to wind up my work, anticipating our return to the States later in July. One young man in particular warmed my heart. His father, a Kenyan political leader, had brought his son into the hospital at the insistence of a veteran missionary. The young man had been born with Erbs palsy of the right shoulder, causing paralysis of the muscles with severe loss of motion. After examination I recommended surgery involving the release of soft tissues. This was easily accomplished, much to the delight of the patient and his father. After a couple of weeks of vigorous exercise, this young man's shoulder had improved noticeably. To my delight, this patient became a believer in Jesus Christ during his hospital stay. I was thrilled to have a part in the calling of another African into God's worldwide family.

Meantime, I found myself still involved in a lot of other work besides that relating to surgery. During the rainy season here in July we were finding it especially difficult to get clothing dry after washing, both at home and at the hospital. Our new Maytag drier had not functioned since the first month of use. Janet had dried our clothing in the sunshine. But now she had too little sunshine. So, finding the instructions ("if all else fails," they say, "read the instructions"), I read with great interest that our problem possibly was nothing more serious than a clogged filter. Dismantling the apparatus, I discovered lint packed so solid that it literally looked like a felt filter over the exhaust. Removing this packed lint repaired the drier. Now, at least, the next occupants of the house would have the benefit of a little-used Maytag drier.

At the hospital, a drier problem developed that could not be so easily solved. Since my Kombi was the only one available, I agreed to transport the hospital laundry to the Rift Valley Academy drier. Little did I realize that this would entail at least half a dozen trips. The African laundry personnel chuckled at seeing the bone doctor working as their laundry truckdriver!

My last official work in Kenya as a surgeon involved one of our AIM missionaries who had been badly injured in Uganda. Ted Crossmen had surprised thieves (and himself) at the mission headquarters, and they attacked him with clubs. A radio call brought the news that Ted and his wife were being flown in by East African Airlines. Canceling all my hospital work, I turned my Kombi into an ambulance by removing all of the back seats and placing a foam mattress on the floor. We had no speicific information as to the extent of Ted's injuries. At the airport, Ted, a husky man of about forty-five, was brought out of the plane by wheelchair. He seemed to be in good spirits, despite a badly broken patella, clavicle, and thumb, along with multiple bruises. Moving him gently from the wheelchair into the "ambulance," we made our way back to Kijabe, driving slowly and carefully to avoid bouncing Ted on the floor.

At the hospital we transferred Ted to his bed and made arrangements for laboratory tests, anticipating surgery the next day. On returning to his room, I found this strong, determined missionary literally weeping. Fearing that Ted had taken a sudden turn for the worse, I was relieved when he smiled through his tears, saying "I am weeping for joy, I am so happy to finally be here at the hospital." It had taken him almost four days to make arrangements and travel to Kijabe. It is difficult to realize the frustrations, fear, and anxiety that the injured or sick missionary must have in tryng to obtain adequate medical care. My contact with this strong man with tears on his cheeks gave me further insight into the matter. Patching Ted up the next day seemed like a fitting finale to an exciting year of surgical experiences.

Our year in Africa had given us keen insight to the problems of God's servants. One thing, I found what I had always suspected: they're all very human despite their tremendous spiritual qualities. They are subject to the same accidents, diseases, and problems that plague other men and women. Some have difficult situations with their children, some missionaries being overly busy in the Lord's work to give sufficient love and attention to their families. Bush missionaries in isolated areas face the frustrations and tensions that early Americans must have experienced as they struggled merely to exist. And now here I had encountered a missionary frustrated because he was at a dead-end street in his favorite work.

Yet for all those who show emotional stress and who aren't batting well in facing life's problems, there are many who aren't affected, at least not enought to show it. But by God's grace both groups are making a real contribution in reaching out to needy people and making Christ known. So many could be home working at high-paying jobs, especially those in medical work. As a family we would go back with a knowledge of how to pray for missionaries and with an awareness of needs that could be met with funds—needs such as X-ray equipment for mission hospitals.

We looked forward to getting home and sharing our findings and experiences with groups of Christians with an interest in missions. We hoped we would be able to give a fresh, objective picture of what mission work is all about. Some of us would even be able to rattle off John 3:16 in Swahili, temporarily at least:

> Kwa maana jinsi hii Mungo aliupenda ulimwengu, hata akamtoa mwanawe pekee, Ili kila mtu amwaminiye asipotee, bali awe na uzima wa milele. (Yohana 3:16)

We didn't want to be caught in the predicament of a certain missionary who, the story goes, went home on his first furlough and was asked in a missionary conference to pray in Swahili. Unfortunately he had worked little with the language, being employed at mission headquarters. So rather sheepishly he prayed by counting as high as he could go and then naming as many food items as he could think of, and ending with "Amen." I wouldn't vouch for the veracity of the story; it was one that came up in conversation as we talked with missionaries.

A highlight of our last days in Kenya was a surprise party held for short-termers who were going home. Nettie Sinclair, a veteran missionary from Scotland, disguised the purpose of the party by calling it a celebration of Scottish Independence Day. Being one-quarter Scot, I felt I qualified but was astonished when I realized it was a good-bye for us and a few others. I remember the devotional on the woman who anointed Jesus with expensive perfume (Mark 14:3). "She did what she could," the speaker emphasized. It is so easy to become overwhelmed with the needs on the mission field but "we can only do what we can. We must do our best and leave it with the Lord," was the message in a nutshell.

The last few days involved packing and tying up loose ends. We put the finishing touches on the house, getting it into order for two short-term doctors who would move in soon after our departure. Various missionaries had donated furniture, so the apartments at least had the essentials for comfortable living. In addition, we turned over our Kombi officially to the academy.

As we packed our luggage, I noted that one of Sue's suitcases was still filled with clothes she apparently hadn't worn. She's our girl athlete and had been running around Kijabe in jeans and a Dallas Cowboy football jersey with the number "26" on its front and back. I tended to refer to her as my flankerback. I had heard of kids spending two weeks at camp without unpacking, but I never thought one of my girls would go for a solid year that way! She claims it's not true, but I saw it with my own eyes.

I didn't have as much clothing to pack as I had brought. A young

Christian African noted that he and I were approximately the same size. Much to my pleasant surprise, two of my suits fit him perfectly. I hated to part with these marvelous garments, but my wife nudged me, reminding me that I needed some new suits; so for a few shillings I presented the suits to this beaming young man. Noting that his wife was also the size of Janet, he inquired about a sweater as well as a coat for her. Janet came forth with both, much to his delight.

Saying good-bye to all of our friends at Kijabe, and especially at the hospital and academy, brought lumps to our throats. But it was great at last to be going home.

Since Sandy and Debbie had returned to the States ahead of us, there were only nine of us returning together. We had twelve large pieces of luggage, plus twenty-three carry-ons. As we stood in line awaiting the check-in at the airport, a voice announced that only one carry-on per person would be allowed. This caused temporary panic. Beth, our sixteen-year-old, hurried into the ladies' room and put on all of the clothing she could possibly wear. When she walked out, she had a gait similar to that of a penguin. But her little scheme to save me money and guarantee that she had all her clothes along proved unnecessary. The rest of us walked onto the plane with our carry-ons, and nothing more was said about limiting the number. Paul carried the largest carry-ons, plus a duffel bag and a sewing machine. All of our children were a sight to behold. Even veteran missionaries, who are used to odd sights, pulled out cameras to snap pictures of the strange group of short-termers.

A stewardess found us nine seats together directly over the wing, and we had ample room for our multiple carry-ons. Since Janet seemed quite tired, I placed her to my right and Jenny to my left. During the eight-hour flight, Jenny took a nap for about an hour. The other seven hours she talked to me constantly. With this barrage of chatter from our youngest, I was almost ready for earplugs.

Landing at Brussels, we checked our large suitcases through and went to pick up the Volkswagen bus our travel agent had reserved for us. We found the reservations hadn't gone through, and neither had our hotel accommodations. I felt as veteran missionaries must feel when they come back and face the realities of civilized life. Happily, another rental agency had a Volkswagen bus available and we finally found a hotel with rooms for us. The night cost a hundred dollars, but with everyone so tired, it was well worth the cost!

Though it was a relief again to be driving on the right side of the road, we still had our problems. In addition to having nine people jammed into the vehicle, the highway signs were not all in English, and rain made driving somewhat difficult. Having heard of a hotel operated by the Salvation Army, a favorite stop for missionaries, we elected to drive to Amsterdam and stay there. This proved to be considerably under one hundred dollars and made me happy for that reason alone.

But our first night in Amsterdam will live forever in our memories. The streets were crowded with shoppers and people doing the town, including those drawn to pornographic shops, of which there were many. We were enjoying window-shopping, strolling in and out of stores. From time to time I would count my kids, as I often do when we are out together. We turned down a side street away from the mainstream of humanity, when suddenly I realized one child was missing. Our eight-year-old Krissy had vanished! I turned and quickly retraced my steps to the intersection, I looked up and down the sidewalk. No Krissy! I nearly panicked. Was our trip going to end in tragedy? Little Krissy did not know the name of our hotel—I didn't even know it myself; I just knew how to get there.

By this time other members of the family, concern on all faces, had joined me. We stepped out of the surge of people and sent up an SOS to God. "O Lord, you know where Krissy is this very moment. Keep her safe, Help us find her quickly." I then sent our kids out two by two in various directions, with instructions to meet back beneath a certain huge flashing sign in twenty minutes. It was a starkly real reenactment of Jesus' story of the shepherd's search for one lost sheep—and our Krissy was the lost sheep.

Perhaps fifteen minutes passed as Janet and I searched in the vicinity of the flashing sign. My throat grew tighter and my mouth drier as I looked for the familiar face of our blue-eyed, pink-cheeked Krissy. I don't know when I had prayed more diligently than during those moments, unless it was months before when the rat bit our Jenny and she couldn't tolerate the rabies shots.

Suddenly Krissy was found. A great burden rolled from me. Judy spotted her completely unconcerned, absorbed in looking into store windows. Krissy's attitude amazed me. It was as if to say, "Me lost? You were the ones who were lost. I thought the rest of you were in a store and would soon be along."

Making our way back to the hotel, we passed through several places where there were houses of ill repute. Attractive women stood in doorways and on doorsteps. Janet expressed amazement at how pretty and young some of these girls were. Feeling that this would be a good lesson for our children, we described the profession of prostitutes and pointed out that the Bible speaks against sex outside of marriage. It proved a real lesson for ten-year-old Jimmy, at least. "I always thought a prostitute was a girl prophet!" he said in all seriousness.

At 7:30 P.M., July 30, 1974, our plane touched down at Chicago-O'Hare. It was thrilling to have about forty friends and relatives, including grandpa and grandma Orr, waiting to greet us with hugs and kisses galore. But it was in some respects anticlimactic. An experience we had our last day in Amsterdam had already given us the feeling we were home. Driving along, we had spied a familiar sign, the golden arch of McDonald's. "Hey, kids," I had exclaimed, "we're running short on time. We have tickets for the museum. Which shall it be—the museum or McDonald's?" Guess which won—by a landslide. Moments later we were enjoying American-style hamburgers, french fries, and malteds. What a way to end the greatest year of our lives!

Epilogue

All in all, our year in Africa isn't something I would want to repeat right away, but as a family we recommend such an experience to all able and with faith enough to give God a time of short-term missionary service.

I saw repeatedly how God used previous knowledge, little techniques I had learned perhaps early in my practice, to enable me to make a real contribution on the mission field in Kenya.

I firmly believe God has a plan for my life and has thoroughly prepared me for that plan, which was service in Kenya in 1973–1974.

On safari, our kids were exposed to a real missionary situation. They saw missionaries as they are and Africans in their need. Some of the older kids are thinking seriously of missionary service.

Would Janet be willing to return to Africa? She says, "I'm very happy here at home; yet I was happy in Africa. My life is bound up in serving my family and their needs and taking care of my husband. I just love doing these things and serving the Lord. So it doesn't matter where I live, whether in the United States or in Africa or some other country."

Sandy, our eldest, is serving in Kenya right now. Returning home ahead of the family, she fell in love with a young missionary, Steve Morad of Gibbsboro, New Jersey, who was on the plane with her. He had been in our home several times, but it took the time on the plane to cause a romance to blossom. They were married in Wheaton on April 19, 1975, and returned to Kenya, where both continued teaching at Rift Valley Academy. They were expecting their first baby as this book was being written. Beth was planning to go back to Kenya to be with Sandy and help out.

Debbie, now studying microbiology at Colorado State University, says she would be willing to be a missionary somewhere, but Africa isn't her life-style. She would rather serve God in the United States.

Paul, who was named "outstanding senior" and won the "competitive spirit" award in his final year of high school, especially has his thoughts turned toward Africa. A freshman in Wheaton College, he is thinking of becoming a missionary teacher, or possibly a missionary doctor. Prior to entering Wheaton, he returned to Africa to play basketball with the Venture for Victory team, giving testimony at half-time concerning God's working in his life.

Beth says she has missions in perspective now. "I used to hear missionaries speak in Sunday school and thought you had to get some terrible feeling in the pit of your stomach to be called to serve God on the mission field," she says. "You were made to feel guilty if you didn't want to go into the unknown. Now I know what missionary work is like, and I wouldn't be at all adverse to going."

Both Judy and Sue are interested in returning as missionaries. Jimmy, Krissy, and Jenny frequently have asked if and when we are returning to Africa. They enjoyed the individual attention provided by their schoolteachers and developed very close friendships with their classmates.

Steve Ross, Paul's buddy, who was selected by his senior class as one of two class speakers at graduation, has his heart set on being a missionary pilot, a direct outgrowth of his months in Kenya. Interestingly, Steve had learned that pilot Arnie Newman had attended Wheaton College. Not only had he lived in the same house before Steve's family moved into it; he had even slept in the same room. Steve caught the vision from Arnie. Now in Wheaton College, he plans to transfer to Moody Bible Institute, Chicago, where he hopes to enroll in that school's missionary aviation program.

Our African safari may have seemed to be the craziest thing I have ever done in my life, but it *was* a once in a lifetime experience!

Bibliography

Adamson, Joy. *The Peoples of Kenya*. New York: Harcourt, Brace & World, 1967.

Cleare, John. *Mountains*. New York: Crown, 1975.

Leslie-Melville, Betty & Jock. *Elephant Have Right of Way*. New York: Doubleday, 1973.

Mason, Gene W. *Minus Three*. Englewood Cliffs, N. J.: Prentice-Hall, 1970.

Pearson, John. *Wildlife & Safari in Kenya*. Nairobi, Kenya: East African Publishing House, 1967.

Petersen, William J. *Another Hand on Mine*. New York: McGraw-Hill, 1967.

Edgar Monsanto. Queeny, "Spearing Lions with Africa's Masai." *National Geographic*, October 1954.

Richardson, Kenneth. *Garden of Miracles*. London: Victory Press, 1968.

Roberts, John S. *A Land Full of People: Life in Kenya Today*. New York: Praeger, 1967.

Short Stories of Ernest Hemingway. New York: Charles Scribner's Sons, 1938.

World Book, vol. 11. Chicago: Field Enterprises, 1969.